1 + 2 TIMOTHY

THE CLARITY YOU NEED WHEN LIFE FEELS CHAOTIC, CONFUSING AND OUT OF CONTROL

Written by Catherine Martinez and designed by Stephanie Norton
Copyright © 2024 by Proverbs 31 Ministries
All Scripture quotations are English Standard Version (ESV) unless otherwise noted.

We must exchange whispers with God before shouts with the world.

LYSA TERKEURST

Pair your study guide with the First 5 mobile app!

This study guide is designed to accompany your study of Scripture in the First 5 mobile app. You can use it as a standalone study or as an accompanying guide to the daily content within First 5.

First 5 is a free mobile app developed by Proverbs 31 Ministries to transform your daily time with God.

Go to the app store on your smartphone, download the First 5 app, and create a free account!

WWW.FIRST5.ORG

WELCOME TO 1 + 2 TIMOTHY

Dear friend,

Once I met a man who shared his testimony of how Jesus saved him from sin. He had been entrenched in the false religion of Voodoo and evil practices, but when Christ changed his heart, he put the lies of his former life in the past. I'll never forget his simple but wise advice: "Stand on the Truth! Stand on the Truth!"

As I've studied 1 and 2 Timothy, I've been moved to tears multiple times by how the Apostle Paul encouraged Timothy to stand on the Truth too. Timothy was more than just Paul's co-worker, a fellow missionary spreading the gospel of Jesus. Timothy was like a son to Paul (1 Timothy 1:2; 2 Timothy 1:2; Philippians 2:22). And like a father passing on an inheritance of his life's work, Paul passed on to Timothy the most valuable thing he had: *the Truth of the gospel of Jesus Christ.*

Timothy was in a challenging situation. He was living in Ephesus, but many in the church there had lost their way and were teaching ideas contrary to the gospel that salvation comes by grace through faith in Jesus Christ alone. These lies caused chaos and confusion among God's people, leading many astray. But Paul encouraged Timothy to minister in Ephesus, fight the good fight of faith (1 Timothy 6:12), and guard the gospel Truth (1 Timothy 6:20).

Maybe you relate to Timothy and feel like you're living in chaos and confusion; I know I do some days. The world is always sending us messages about what we need to do, who we need to be, and what we need to believe. But instead of clarity, we get chaos that makes us feel out of control.

We may not even realize it, but the lies of the world can become the lens through which we view our lives and can get mixed in with our fundamental

> *"Jesus brings the clarity our hearts crave."*

beliefs, including what we believe about God. Even though times and cultures change, Satan is still using the same old formula to try to trap us: lies that cause destruction.

The enemy wants you to believe that God isn't good, holy or just. He wants you to believe that Jesus' sacrifice wasn't enough to save you and that you must somehow atone for yourself. He wants you to believe that you cannot effectively share the gospel with your friends and neighbors.

But the enemy is a liar.

Praise God that our Savior is the Truth! As we study 1 and 2 Timothy together, we'll learn that the best way to combat lies is with His Word. Jesus brings the clarity our hearts crave. He promises that knowing the Truth will set us free (John 8:32).

On each day of this journey, we'll identify a common lie and confront it with God's Truth that will bring clarity. Along the way, as God's Word helps you strike down confusing lies you've been believing in your own life, you can write His Truth in the margins and consider memorizing some key scriptures to help you defy the enemy's deceptions.

I'm thrilled you decided to study 1 and 2 Timothy. We will never regret one moment we spend in God's Word — so let's get started.

Stand on the Truth, my friend,

Catherine

AUTHOR AND DATE OF 1 + 2 TIMOTHY

The books of 1 and 2 Timothy were originally written as "pastoral epistles," or letters offering guidance to early Christian pastors about how to lead and shepherd their churches in the first century. First Timothy 1:1 quickly reveals the letter's author: *"Paul, an apostle of Christ Jesus by command of God our Savior and of Christ Jesus our hope."*

For most of Church history, Paul has been credited as the author of 1 and 2 Timothy, though some scholars in the last 200 years have questioned his authorship.[1] The reasoning of these scholars is that the language and topics explored in 1 and 2 Timothy are sometimes different from the content of Paul's other epistles (Colossians, Ephesians, Galatians, etc.). Also, there have been some difficulties in fitting 1 and 2 Timothy chronologically into the narrative of Acts, a book that chronicles much of Paul's missionary activity.

However, most scholars note that the differences in Paul's word choices can be explained by context and subject matter. In 1 and 2 Timothy, Paul was addressing Timothy's specific issues in Ephesus (which explains why he did not address some of the themes from his other letters) and spoke in a personal tone to his close friend. We also know Luke was with Paul while he wrote 2 Timothy (2 Timothy 4:11), so he may have served as a scribe for Paul, and that could explain some differences in writing style.

To account for how 1 and 2 Timothy fit into the chronology of Acts, it's probable that both letters were written after Paul's release from his first Roman imprisonment in Acts 28, and then Paul was later arrested again. As the *Holman Bible Handbook* says, "There is no compelling reason to deny the claim of Paul's authorship."[2]

Most scholars estimate that 1 Timothy was written around A.D. 62-64, perhaps from Macedonia, while most believe 2 Timothy was written around A.D. 62-67 from a prison in Rome.[3]

THE WORST OF SINNERS:
More About Paul

Paul of Tarsus, also called Saul, was a Jewish man from the tribe of Benjamin (Philippians 3:5). He was born a Roman citizen, so many scholars believe his family may have had significant social standing. At the age of 13, a Jewish boy becomes a bar mitzvah (which means "son of a commandment"), and some scholars believe this would've been the age at which Paul went to Jerusalem to be *"educated at the feet of Gamaliel"* (Acts 22:3), a prestigious Jewish teacher.[1] Due to this education Paul received, he knew the law of the Old Testament inside and out.

Paul was also a fierce persecutor of the early Christian Church. He was fiercely committed to the old covenant of the law and did not believe in Jesus' new covenant of grace. He approved when Stephen (a church leader) was martyred, and Paul *"was ravaging the church … [and] entering house after house, he dragged off men and women and committed them to prison"* (Acts 8:1-3).

But that's when Jesus graciously called Paul to follow Him. On the road to Damascus, Jesus appeared in a bright light from heaven and asked, *"'Saul, Saul, why are you persecuting me?' And [Saul] said, 'Who are you, Lord?' And he said, 'I am Jesus, whom you are persecuting'"* (Acts 9:4-5). Later, scales fell from Paul's eyes as he saw the truth about Jesus. He was filled with the Holy Spirit and baptized (Acts 9:17-18).

Because of his personal call and commission by Christ to take the gospel to the world, Paul identified himself as *"an **apostle** of Christ Jesus by command of God our Savior and of Christ Jesus"* (1 Timothy 1:1, emphasis added). Theologian R.C. Sproul says, "The apostles were called and commissioned directly by Christ and spoke with His authority."[2] Paul's status and authority as an apostle is a crucial topic in 1 and 2 Timothy.

When Jesus called Paul to Himself, He also said, *"I will show him how much he must suffer for the sake of my name"* (Acts 9:16). And Paul did suffer throughout his ministry. The persecutor became the persecuted one, and Paul experienced multiple imprisonments, a shipwreck, riots, periods of abandonment and countless other trials (2 Corinthians 11:16-33). But all this suffering was worth it to Paul. He considered himself the worst of sinners but was endlessly grateful that he had experienced the radical grace and love of Jesus Christ (1 Timothy 1:15).

Jesus entrusted the gospel to Paul. Paul entrusted it to Timothy, and it is entrusted to us today. The gospel message of God's unfathomable, inexhaustible grace is the most precious thing we can pass on to others.

History suggests Paul was martyred for his faith shortly after writing 2 Timothy, likely from a dungeon-like prison cell in Rome. He *"fought the good fight … finished the race … kept the faith"* until the end (2 Timothy 4:7). As we go through our study, let's remember that Paul was willing to suffer for the sake of the gospel because he had a front-row seat to its power in his own life. Jesus' grace and mercy transformed the worst of sinners into a mighty warrior of the faith — and He is still transforming hearts today.

WHO WAS TIMOTHY?
Paul's Relatable Missionary Assistant

As we'll see throughout our study, Paul and Timothy had a remarkable friendship based on sharing the gospel and fortifying the Church, with Paul acting as a spiritual father and mentor to Timothy. But who was Timothy, and what was the backstory to his great friendship with Paul?

Paul first met Timothy in Acts 16:1-5, when Paul was ministering in Lystra and Derbe. Timothy's mother, Eunice, was a Jewish Christian, and his father was a gentile, meaning Timothy was of mixed racial descent. Timothy's grandmother Lois and his mother were strong believers, raising him in a household of faith (2 Timothy 1:5).

Paul wanted Timothy to accompany him on his missionary journey, but Timothy was not circumcised, as all law-abiding Jews were according to the Old Testament (Genesis 17). Paul was worried that Timothy being uncircumcised may offend Jewish people to whom they would minister. So even though we know circumcision is not required for Christians because Jesus has fulfilled the law on our behalf (Acts 15:1-35), Paul circumcised Timothy so as not to create an obstacle for the Jews they would meet as they declared the gospel on their journey (Acts 16:3).

Bible scholar William Marty says, "Paul had Timothy circumcised not as a precondition for salvation but as an outward sign of the Abrahamic covenant."[1] Like Paul, Timothy was willing to become all things to all people so some may be saved (1 Corinthians 9:19-23), which meant he was willing to do anything to get people to listen to the gospel.

Timothy accompanied Paul on his missionary journeys in the book of Acts and is mentioned in other epistles as one of Paul's trusted assistants and representatives, visiting the churches in Corinth (1 Corinthians 4:17), Philippi (Philippians 1:1) and Thessalonica (1 Thessalonians 1:1). Like Paul, Timothy was imprisoned at one point but then released (Hebrews 13:23). When we meet him in 1 and 2 Timothy, Paul had sent him to minister to the churches in Ephesus.

Timothy had many personal characteristics that made him both admirable and relatable. We know he was a man of compassion and humility: Paul told the church at Philippi, *"I have no one like him, who will be genuinely concerned for your welfare … you know Timothy's proven worth, how as a son with a father he has served with me in the gospel"* (Philippians 2:20-22). Timothy cared deeply about the spiritual well-being of others and had his own *"sincere faith"* (2 Timothy 1:5).

We also know Timothy had struggles, including a stomach issue (1 Timothy 5:23); fear and timidity (2 Timothy 1:7); and bouts of discouragement, low confidence and spiritual warfare. Paul had to remind him *"God gave us a spirit not of fear but of power and love and self-control"* (2 Timothy 1:7).

It would have been tempting for Timothy to give up on the Ephesian church, where it seemed there were more spiritual issues than spiritual victories and growth. Still, Paul encouraged Timothy to *"fight the good fight of the faith"* (1 Timothy 6:12) and reminded him that God called him to this work (1 Timothy 4:14). Timothy wasn't perfect, but he was faithful, humble, and willing to grow and learn for the sake of the gospel. Timothy's struggles also show us that God can use ordinary people for His extraordinary purposes.

As we study these letters, let's try to imagine ourselves in Paul and Timothy's shoes. Like Paul, we can encourage younger or newer Christians in their faith and point them toward the gospel. Like Timothy, we can seek godly discipleship in our lives and be humble enough to learn.

WHY DID PAUL WRITE 1 + 2 TIMOTHY?

PAUL'S PURPOSE

Paul was concerned about the health of the churches in Ephesus, so while he was in Macedonia, he sent Timothy to respond to the crisis. Many scholars believe Timothy was not the pastor of one congregation but oversaw all of the pastors of individual house churches in Ephesus.

Paul specifically told Timothy his purpose for writing to him: *"I hope to come to you soon, but I am writing these things to you so that, if I delay, you may know how one ought to behave in the household of God, which is the church of the living God, a pillar and buttress of the truth"* (1 Timothy 3:14-15).

False doctrines, which are any teachings that do not preach the gospel of salvation by grace through faith in Jesus Christ, had overtaken the leaders of the Ephesian churches. The exact nature of these heresies is unclear, but through Paul's writing, we can see they involved asceticism (extreme, unnecessary self-denial for religious purposes) and misuse of the Old Testament law. We know false teachings were causing chaos among the believers, distorting the gospel, and causing division. So Paul gave Timothy an assignment to teach the Ephesians how to behave in church and how to keep the Truth of Christ at the center of their teaching.

ADDITIONAL CONTEXT ABOUT EPHESUS

Before writing 1 and 2 Timothy, Paul had a long history in Ephesus, having spent an estimated three years establishing the church there (A.D. 52-55) and having written a letter to the Ephesian church in A.D. 62 (which we know as the biblical book of Ephesians). Acts 19:20 tells us *"the word of the Lord continued to increase and prevail mightily"* in Ephesus, leading many to turn to Christ.

Yet this also led to an incident, recorded in Acts 19:21-40, between Paul and a group of craftsmen who made their living from selling idols at the temple of Artemis (aka the Roman fertility goddess Diana). Each year, people came from all over the region to worship at the temple of Artemis, buying idols — but Paul's message of Truth was bound to put the idol-makers out of

MAP OF ANCIENT EPHESUS
(Modern-Day Turkey)[1]

business. A riot ensued at the Ephesian theater, a structure that could hold over 20,000 people and where locals regularly held town meetings and gatherings. Shortly after, Paul left Ephesus for Macedonia.

This incident gives us a glimpse into Ephesian culture at the time, which was entrenched in idolatry and spiritual warfare. Declaring God's Truth in this environment would have felt overwhelming and dangerous, *but that's why it was so important.* The Church needed to be *"a pillar and buttress of the truth"* (1 Timothy 3:15), with believers sharing the message of Jesus with their friends, neighbors and the next generation.

When 2 Timothy was written, Timothy may have still been in Ephesus, but Paul was likely in a prison in Rome because of his missionary activity, awaiting execution. It is believed his execution happened under the rule of Nero (A.D. 54–68), which was an intense period of Christian persecution.

GODLINESS WITH CONTENTMENT

1 TIMOTHY

It may seem 1 Timothy was primarily written for church leaders since there are many specifics about church order and leadership — but this letter is also for the benefit of all of God's people. We all have a crucial role to play in the life and mission of the Church. First Timothy also gives us helpful instructions for how to live out our faith; the *ESV Study Bible* says the theme of 1 Timothy "is that the gospel leads to practical, visible change in the lives of those who believe it."[1]

All followers of Jesus are called to total life transformation that produces godliness. Godly churches are made up of once ungodly people who have been redeemed and set free from sin through Jesus' magnificent gift of grace and mercy. Along these lines, here are a few significant themes to look out for in the book of 1 Timothy:

- **HOW TO DEAL WITH FALSE TEACHERS.** Timothy faced a significant threat of false teachers in the Ephesian church. Paul gave him instructions on how to deal with these teachers with grace and truth, and his words also equip us today to look out for teachings that claim to be Christian but run contrary to Scripture.

- **THE IMPORTANCE OF SHARING THE GOSPEL.** Paul shared his testimony and encouraged the Church, then and now, to pray for the salvation of all people.

- **GOSPEL-CENTERED GODLINESS.** The gospel transforms our hearts and inspires us to put our faith into action, including acts of mercy and caring for those in need. In 1 Timothy, words relating to "godliness" are mentioned 10 times![2]

- **APPROPRIATE CORPORATE WORSHIP.** Paul gave specific instructions about church order and the marks of a functional local church, which we can contextualize for our churches today.

- **QUALITIES OF GODLY CHURCH LEADERS.** Church leaders are to exhibit godly character and live lives devoted to the gospel, and believers are to honor and exemplify such leaders.

- **MAINTAINING THE PURITY OF THE GOSPEL.**[3] Paul reminds us the gospel itself is sufficient for salvation; nothing is to be added to it or taken away from it. Fighting for the preservation of the true gospel is the "*good fight*" (1 Timothy 6:12).

IS GREAT GAIN:
Themes in 1 + 2 Timothy

2 TIMOTHY

In Paul's last known letter, it seems appropriate that the overall theme focuses on perseverance in sharing the gospel. Some have said 2 Timothy was like Paul's last will and testament, and he charged Timothy to *"guard the good deposit entrusted to [him]"* (2 Timothy 1:14). Paul was passing on the torch of leadership to the next generation of church leaders, and he encouraged Timothy to continue in ministry after he was gone (2 Timothy 4:7).

In 2 Timothy we will see themes similar to those to 1 Timothy, but here are a few more to look out for as we study:

- **SUFFERING AND PERSEVERANCE.** The Christian life isn't easy, but our suffering is temporary and will pale in comparison to the glory of eternity. Paul persevered and *"finished the race"* of faith God had prepared for him (2 Timothy 4:7), encouraging Timothy and us to do the same.

- **GUARDING THE ORIGINAL, UN-CHANGING GOSPEL MESSAGE.** Again, Paul implored Timothy to guard the gospel — the Truth that Jesus died for our sins and rose again — which means preserving the gospel message over time so believers in all generations may be saved.

- **THE AUTHORITY AND SUFFICIENCY OF SCRIPTURE.** The Word of God is *"breathed out by God"* that we may be *"complete"* and *"equipped for every good work"* (2 Timothy 3:16-17). God's people study and obey His Scriptures!

MAJOR MOMENTS

WEEK ONE

DAY 1 *1 Timothy 1:1-11*
Paul greeted Timothy and warned him about false teachers in the Church.

DAY 2 *1 Timothy 1:12-20*
Paul shared the gospel through his personal testimony.

DAY 3 *1 Timothy 2:1-7*
Paul stressed the importance of praying for all people.

DAY 4 *1 Timothy 2:8-15*
Paul set guidelines for men and women in the Church.

DAY 5 *1 Timothy 3:1-7*
Paul gave qualifications for those serving as elders in the Church.

WEEK TWO

DAY 6 *1 Timothy 3:8-13*
Paul gave qualifications for those who serve as deacons in the Church.

DAY 7 *1 Timothy 3:14-16*
Paul stated his central purpose for writing to Timothy.

DAY 8 *1 Timothy 4:1-5*
Paul said some people will walk away from the faith.

DAY 9 *1 Timothy 4:6-16*
Paul encouraged Timothy to train himself for godliness.

DAY 10 *1 Timothy 5:1-16*
Paul instructed the Church on how to care for each other as God's family.

WEEK THREE

DAY 11 *1 Timothy 5:17-25*
Paul gave instructions regarding care for church elders.

DAY 12 *1 Timothy 6:1-10*
Paul taught that godliness leads to contentment and great gain.

DAY 13 *1 Timothy 6:11-21*
Paul closed his first letter to Timothy with a reminder to fight the good fight of faith.

DAY 14 *2 Timothy 1:1-7*
Paul asserted that the Holy Spirit gives love, power and self-control to followers of Christ.

DAY 15 *2 Timothy 1:8-18*
Paul told Timothy not to be ashamed of the gospel and to share in his suffering.

WEEK FOUR

DAY 16 *2 Timothy 2:1-7*
Paul encouraged Timothy to teach the gospel, using three examples.

DAY 17 *2 Timothy 2:8-13*
Paul urged Timothy to remember Jesus Christ.

DAY 18 *2 Timothy 2:14-19*
Paul said believers are to present ourselves as workers who don't need to be ashamed.

DAY 19 *2 Timothy 2:20-26*
Paul instructed Timothy to pursue righteousness, faith, love and peace.

DAY 20 *2 Timothy 3:1-9*
Paul warned Timothy about the conduct of false teachers in the last days.

WEEK FIVE

DAY 21 *2 Timothy 3:10-17*
Paul declared that all Scripture is breathed out by God.

DAY 22 *2 Timothy 4:1-5*
Paul told Timothy to preach God's Word.

DAY 23 *2 Timothy 4:6-8*
Paul had finished the race and fought the good fight.

DAY 24 *2 Timothy 4:9-18*
Paul gave Timothy instructions to come to him soon.

DAY 25 *2 Timothy 4:19-22*
Paul concluded his second letter with personal greetings.

WEEK One

DAY 1 / 1 TIMOTHY 1:1-11

Paul greeted Timothy and warned him about false teachers in the Church.

Do you ever get discouraged as you try to follow God's good plan but it seems like things go wrong? Maybe you've been doing your best to serve others the way God wants you to, but you don't see the results you hoped for, and you find yourself praying for clarity.

As we kick off our first day of study, we'll see Timothy probably felt the same way about his ministry in Ephesus. He was urged to stay there instead of continuing to Macedonia with Paul, as *"certain persons"* in Ephesus were spreading false teachings and needed correction (1 Timothy 1:3). These issues may have been disheartening, but Paul had a simple, encouraging message for his friend Timothy: "Don't quit!"[1]

> As we dig into 1 and 2 Timothy, how do you hope to be encouraged through this study?

Paul started his letter by reiterating his authority as an apostle, which was given to him directly by God (1 Timothy 1:1), and by reminding Timothy that he was his *"true child in the faith"* (v. 2).

> Paul's letters to Timothy are different from many of his other letters because they are written first and foremost to one person and only secondarily to the Church at large. What does the personal address in verse 2 tell you about how much Timothy meant to Paul?

Paul didn't waste time in getting to the point. Timothy faced a serious threat: False teachers had infiltrated the Church, declaring a *"different doctrine"* than salvation by grace through faith in Christ (1 Timothy 1:3). Instead, they focused on *"myths and endless genealogies"* (v. 4) that led to *"vain discussion"* (v. 6) and promoted controversy and discord within the body of Christ.

We don't know the exact nature of these false teachings, but scholars believe they were an unhealthy form of asceticism, which is extreme self-denial for religious purposes. In another of his letters, Paul said asceticism involved "*severity to the body*" but had "*no value*" as a tool for godly self-control (Colossians 2:23). While self-denial is not a bad thing in and of itself, we can never earn our salvation by abstaining from food, marriage or anything else God has created.

> What did Paul say these false teachings "*promote*" (1 Timothy 1:4)? Why is this such a serious problem?

> How have you seen false teaching cause chaos in your life or the life of a friend or family member? Consider how it can be dangerous to "twist" the gospel even slightly (for example: the idea that Jesus is a good teacher but is not God, the idea that Jesus is one way to God but is not the *only* way, etc.).

The false teachers in Ephesus were also misusing the Old Testament law, with no self-awareness of their error (1 Timothy 1:7). God's law is His perfect standard for all humankind, laid out in the first five books of the Old Testament (also called the Torah), including the Ten Commandments found in Exodus 20. But false teachers were likely leading people down a path of religious legalism, teaching that they could be saved by their own behavior instead of by Christ, who is the only One truly able to keep God's law.

> Fill in the blanks from 1 Timothy 1:5 to learn how and why Timothy needed to confront these false teachers:
>
> "*The aim of our charge is _____ that issues from a _____ _____ and a good _____ and a _____ _____.*"

Timothy was sent to rebuke false teachings not from a heart of judgment or self-righteousness but a heart filled with love. This is an important lesson for us, too, as we seek to be ambassadors of Christ's Truth.

Take a look at 1 Timothy 1:9-10. Who was the law meant for?

If you found yourself cringing while reading the sins on this list, you're not alone. Most cringeworthy is the realization that we *all* were once "*lawless and disobedient*" before we trusted Christ (v. 9). Romans 3:23 tells us, *"All have sinned and fall short of the glory of God."* The law was meant to convict sinners, but it can never save us. It only serves to diagnose the problem: We need Jesus to fulfill the law for us.

Dear friend, if you have placed your faith in Jesus, He has set you free from the bondage of sin and the law. As we end today's study, take a moment to thank Him for the gospel that sets sinners like us free!

Lie that creates chaos:

You can be saved by being a good person or following all the rules.

Truth that brings clarity:

Jesus kept the law perfectly so sinners can be saved by grace through faith in Him.

WHAT IS FALSE DOCTRINE?

We're going to talk frequently about false doctrine and false teachers throughout our study of 1 and 2 Timothy, so it's important to define what these terms mean. For our purposes, a "doctrine" is a belief or set of beliefs taught by God through Scripture and upheld by faithful believers in Jesus. False doctrines are teachings that purposely distort the Truth of Scripture. Likewise, a false teacher is someone whose untrue teachings run contrary to the gospel message. More so than teachers who are spiritually immature or simply do not understand a certain passage of the Bible, false teachers willfully depart from Truth.

It's also important to point out that Christians can have different opinions about some theological topics without falling into the category of heresy or false teaching. An example of varied opinions might be the range of views that Christian denominations hold about baptism. Differing interpretations create distinct church groups or "*factions*" of like-minded believers, as Paul mentions in 1 Corinthians 11:19, but believers who disagree about methods of baptism can still agree on the gospel itself, which unites all followers of Jesus.

The core theological truths of the gospel cannot be negotiated because of their centrality to the Christian faith. These doctrines include: the holy Trinity of God, the virgin birth of Jesus, salvation by grace through faith in Jesus, the deity and sinlessness of Jesus, and the authority and infallibility of the Bible.

The gospel Truth is what Paul says is "*of first importance … that Christ died for our sins in accordance with the Scriptures, that he was buried, [and] that he was raised on the third day in accordance with the Scriptures*" to offer eternal life to all who will believe in Him (1 Corinthians 15:3-4).

DAY 2 / 1 TIMOTHY 1:12-20

Paul shared the gospel through his personal testimony.

Many television commercials use "before" and "after" pictures to prove the effectiveness of the product. The voice-over may go something like this: "Justine used to have yellow, stained teeth, but since trying our patented, teeth-whitening toothpaste, her teeth are white, and her smile glistens!" These commercials may be cheesy, but they have one purpose – to show transformation.

Today's reading is like a set of "before Jesus" and "after Jesus" descriptions of Paul, proving God's grace can transform anyone.

After warning Timothy about false teachers and legalists in yestedoy's scriptures, Paul admitted that he himself was once a *"blasphemer,"* denying Jesus was God; a *"persecutor"* of Christians, putting them to death; and an *"insolent opponent,"* which is another way of saying he was a bully (1 Timothy 1:13). In the book of Acts, we read about a leader in the early Christian Church named Stephen who was sentenced to death by stoning because of his faith, and Paul (also called Saul) approved (Acts 7:58b).

> Read Acts 8:1-3. What do you think motivated Paul's former persecution of the Church? What was the state of his heart?

After he encountered the grace of Jesus (Acts 9), Paul's heart overflowed with faith and love. When we come to faith in Jesus, His grace transforms our hearts too.

> How has the grace and mercy of God transformed your heart? List some specific ways below:

Before I knew Christ, I was ...   *In Christ, I am ...*

Paul declared the gospel message succinctly and humbly: *"Christ Jesus came into the world to save sinners, of whom I am the foremost"* (1 Timothy 1:15). After giving a long list of sins and sinners in 1 Timothy 1:9-10, Paul was saying, "Remember all those sinners I told you about? I'm the worst one." When we realize how much grace and forgiveness God has shown us, we don't have an attitude of judgment toward other people.

> Even though Paul had been a fierce opponent of the gospel, God's grace sought him out, and he *"received mercy because [he] had acted ignorantly in unbelief"* (1 Timothy 1:13). Look at 1 Timothy 1:16. What was God's purpose for showing Paul mercy?

The gospel did what the law could never do: transform Paul's heart and life through the saving grace of Jesus.

> As long as they're alive on earth, no one is beyond the abundant grace and mercy of God. Have you ever been tempted to give up on a friend or family member coming to salvation in Christ? How does Paul's testimony encourage you to continue praying, sharing the gospel and serving this person in Jesus' name?

Paul knew the Good News is precious, so he entrusted it to Timothy. He charged Timothy to confront the false teachers in Ephesus and *"wage the good warfare, holding faith and a good conscience"* (1 Timothy 1:18-19a).

Paul also mentioned two false teachers by name, Hymenaeus and Alexander, saying they had been *"handed over to Satan that they may learn"* (1 Timothy 1:20). Likely this referred to church discipline that would remove them from the fellowship in some way on a temporary basis — until they turned away from their sin in repentance. Similar phrasing is also used in Corinthians 5:5, and though it may sound harsh, let's notice the purpose: *"that his spirit may be saved in the day of the Lord."* This discipline was motivated by love (1 Timothy 1:5), intended to lead the false teachers to repentance.

What does Hebrews 12:6 say about God's loving discipline? How has God's discipline led to repentance in your own life?

Friend, God's discipline and correction are expressions of His work in our lives. As we close today's session, let's ask God to open our eyes to how His discipline has graced us and the people we love.

Lie that creates chaos:

Some people are beyond God's redemption.

Truth that brings clarity:

Even the worst of sinners can be transformed by the gospel when they trust in Christ.

DAY 3 / 1 TIMOTHY 2:1-7

Paul stressed the importance of praying for all people.

You may have heard the joking phrase, "Behind every good man is a good woman." But when we look at today's Bible passage, Paul essentially said, on a more serious note, "Behind every good church is a group of prayer warriors."

After Paul charged Timothy to combat false teaching in Ephesus and encourage believers who were living in sin to repent, he gave the foundation for healthy church practice: *"First of all, then, I urge that supplications, prayers, intercessions, and thanksgivings be made for all people"* (1 Timothy 2:1). A healthy church is a praying church that has a heart for all people, whomever they may be.

> What specific groups of people does Paul say we should pray for in 1 Timothy 2:2? Why is this hard to do sometimes?

Followers of Christ are to pray for anyone in authority, not just government leaders. From our boss to local business leaders to people with high levels of influence in society, we are to pray for these leaders so *"we may lead a peaceful and quiet life, godly and dignified in every way"* (1 Timothy 2:2). Leaders can influence large groups of people either positively or negatively, which can make it either harder or easier to live our lives in a way that is pleasing to God.

But this doesn't mean we pray for such people just because they have influence — we pray because *all people* are created in the image of God, who wants to save their souls.

> Do you find it easier to pray for authority figures who follow Jesus or for those who don't? Why do you think it's important to pray for both, according to verses 3-6?

All people, from world leaders to children, need Jesus. And God *"desires all people to be saved and to come to the knowledge of the truth"* (1 Timothy 2:4). This should not be misunderstood as universalism (the idea that all people will be saved whether they believe in Jesus or not) nor as pluralism (the idea that there are many ways to salvation). We know salvation comes only through faith in Jesus alone. What this passage clearly teaches is that God's offer of salvation is extended to all people because God invites everyone to believe in Christ.

Paul gives three truths of the gospel in 1 Timothy 2:5-6. Fill in the blanks based on what you find in these verses:

1. There is only _____ God.

2. There is only _____ mediator, and His name is _____.
   He bridges the gap between us and God; nobody else can do it!

3. Jesus gave Himself as a _____ for all people. He paid the price for our sins with His life!

There is only one way to salvation. Jesus Himself said, *"I am the way, and the truth, and the life. No one comes to the Father except through me"* (John 14:6). Why do you think this truth can be hard to accept? Why is it worth accepting?

Friend, Jesus came to save you. He also came to save your neighbor, the cashier at the grocery store, your supervisor at work.

To end today's session, write down the name of someone in your life who does not know Jesus yet. Pray this person would *"come to the knowledge of the truth"* found in Jesus alone (1 Timothy 2:4). This is a prayer with eternal significance!

Lie that creates chaos:

There is more than one way to salvation.

Truth that brings clarity:

Jesus is the one mediator who can bring reconciliation between God and human beings.

DAY 4 / 1 TIMOTHY 2:8-15

Paul set guidelines for men and women in the Church.

Proverbs 16:18 says, *"Pride goes before destruction, and a haughty spirit before a fall."* In Ephesus, pride had seemingly become a problem for both men and women in the church, causing chaos in the congregation. This pride came out in different ways, with the men struggling with anger (1 Timothy 2:8) and the women struggling with immodesty and lack of self-control (1 Timothy 2:9-11).

Whatever our own struggles with pride look like, we can learn from today's passage too. We'll find there is a range of theological interpretations to consider about the roles of men and women in the Church, but as we read, it's important to remember that prideful hearts were and are a root cause of problems for everyone. As we study different opinions, let's keep a spirit of humility, as Paul encourages.

First, Paul gave men in the Ephesian church the directive to *"pray, lifting holy hands without anger or quarreling"* (1 Timothy 2:8). Paul wanted the men to solve their arguments through a humble posture of prayer — which is often the best thing any of us can do when we have disagreements with our brothers and sisters in Christ.

> What are some issues God may be calling you to stop fighting over and turn over to Him in humble prayer today?

While the men in Ephesus were apparently fighting, the women seemed to be trying to attract attention or gain influence through their appearance, and many scholars believe this included flaunting their wealth (with *"gold or pearls or costly attire"* [v. 9]). Paul was not necessarily prohibiting all Christian women from braiding their hair or wearing jewelry, nor was he establishing a universal "dress code" for all churches for the rest of time. But he was warning against excessive adornment, especially in a culture that was riddled with sexual immorality. Christian women are to clothe themselves in virtues that never go out of style: godliness and good works (v. 10).

> Read Colossians 3:12-14. What are all God's people to *"put on"* or clothe themselves with? How can you clothe yourself in this way?

The world sees our appearance, but the Lord knows what's going on in our hearts (1 Samuel 16:7). How does focusing on the state of our heart over our outward appearance change our priorities?

First Timothy 2:11-15 continues Paul's guidance for men and women, though theologians and church denominations may differ in their interpretations of some details. The Greek word translated as *"exercise authority"* in 1 Timothy 2:12 is *authenteo*, and this is the only place it's used in the Bible, which makes it difficult to get additional context from other passages.[1] We can also note that these verses talk about the authority of women *in the Church;* the authority of women outside the Church is a separate topic from what is discussed in 1 Timothy 2. For example, there is no argument from 1 Timothy 2 against men submitting to female bosses or female police officers.

With that in mind, there are several different ideas about what authority might practically look like in the Church, including the following generalized views:

1. Some interpret this passage as saying women are not permitted to hold **any roles** of authority over men in the Church, though they can teach other women or children. Often cited in accordance with this is Titus 2:3-5. Paul's explanation that *"Adam was formed first"* and that *"she will be saved through childbearing"* (1 Timothy 2:13-15) is said to reference how God designated different roles for men and women — not only in marriage but within God's family, the Church — from the very beginning.[2]

2. Some interpret this passage as asserting that women are permitted to hold **most roles** in the Church, except the role of pastor. This would suggest women can be church staff members, leaders, ministers or teachers under the authority of a male leader or pastor. People who lean toward this interpretation may believe a woman can teach the Bible in church or other spiritual contexts, even with men in the audience, but should not teach as the leader of a local congregation.[3]

3. Other interpretations suggest that women are permitted to hold **all roles** in the Church, including leadership, serving, teaching and pastoral roles. Believers who align with this view may interpret Paul's prohibition in verse 12 as specifically directed toward Ephesian women who were part of that local church's issue with false teaching. At Artemis' temple, women were the chief leaders, and Paul may have been warning the Ephesians not to follow the pagan cultural norm of females leading religious worship. They didn't worship Artemis anymore but the one true God.[4]

Bible teacher Tara-Leigh Cobble says, "Even among Spirit-filled people, it's challenging to reach total agreement on what Scripture means here and whether it applies universally or not."[5] But while followers of Christ may hold different views on this topic, we can all agree that both men and women are created in the image of God, and while our roles may be different, our value and dignity is the same (Genesis 1:27).

Finally, when reading verses like 1 Timothy 2:11, we may think of authority as a "greater" role than submission. But Jesus gives us the perfect example of humbly submitting to God in His humanity, even as He is equal with the Father in His divinity (John 10:30; Matthew 28:18).

> Read Matthew 26:39 and John 6:38-40, and note what you learn about Jesus' submission in His humanity:

Through His life, death and resurrection, Jesus showed us that godly authority requires sacrifice and that submission requires humble strength (John 10:17-18; Philippians 2:8). How does this example help us *"submi[t] to one another out of reverence for Christ"* (Ephesians 5:21) in the context of the Church?

Dear sister, let's make clothing our hearts in humility a priority today — we will never regret a humble attitude.

Lie that creates chaos:

Being humble will never get you anywhere; you must put yourself first to be successful.

Truth that brings clarity:

A gentle, humble and quiet spirit is most precious to God. The world may not see it, but God does!

TOUGH TOPICS IN 1 TIMOTHY:
Are Women Saved in Childbearing?

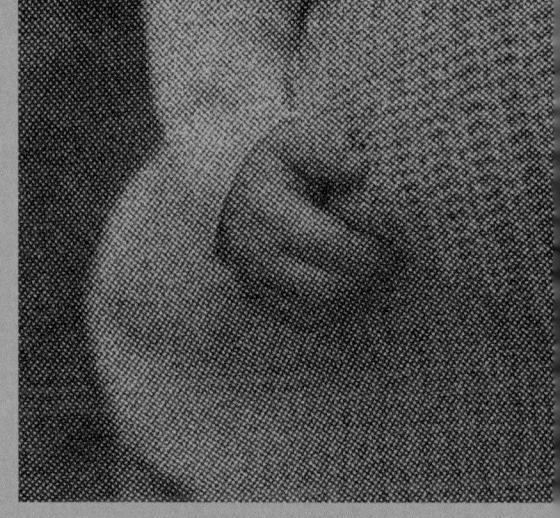

First Timothy 2:15 has astounded theologians for centuries: "*Yet she will be saved through childbearing—if they continue in faith and love and holiness, with self-control.*" There is widespread agreement that this does not mean women are granted spiritual salvation in childbearing, as we know that salvation for both men and women is by grace through faith in Jesus alone. There is nothing we can do to earn our salvation, including bearing children (Galatians 3:26-29; Ephesians 2:8).

With that in mind, here are a few theories about Paul's possible meanings in 1 Timothy 2:15, although most scholars do not take an adamant position:

1. This verse may have messianic undertones of Genesis 3:15, where God promised to send a Redeemer through the offspring of a woman (Eve) — thus, in one sense, humanity has been saved through childbearing because of Jesus' birth.

2. In first-century Ephesus, childbearing was riskier than it is today — women didn't know if they would make it out alive. To try to ensure a healthy delivery, it would have been tempting for a pregnant Christian woman to fall prey to the cultural pressure of making a sacrifice to Artemis, a goddess who promised fertility. Paul may have been saying that women could hope to survive childbearing not because of Artemis, a false god, but because of the true God who is sovereign over the outcome of all things.

3. Another interpretation could be that by raising children at home, which most mothers did in first-century societies, women could be protected or spared from some kinds of worldly corruption.[1]

DAY 5 / 1 TIMOTHY 3:1-7

Paul gave qualifications for those serving as elders in the Church.

If you've ever applied for a job, chances are that you had to submit references to your potential employer. Good references will vouch for your character and skill and explain why you're a great fit for the job. In today's reading, Paul was concerned with the personal character of overseers in the Church — he wanted to make sure they had references!

Paul had just finished explaining specific ways men and women can bless the Church by demonstrating humility. Now he pointed particularly to local church leaders, saying humility is to be part of their lifestyle. With this in view, Paul described the personal qualifications required for *"the office of overseer"* (1 Timothy 3:1).

The Greek word for "overseer" is *episkopos*, which is one of several words used in the New Testament to describe the church leadership position many scholars regard as interchangeable with the role of *presbyteroi* ("elder").[1] Elders may not be literally the oldest members of a church, but they are spiritually mature leaders, pastors or shepherds of local congregations (1 Peter 5:1-3). Bible teacher Phillip Jensen writes, "The task is noble. The people doing it must match its nobility."[2]

Paul said overseers *"must be above reproach"* (1 Timothy 3:2), which is another way of saying righteous, not living in a hypocritical way. The Greek word for *"above reproach"* is *anepilempton*, and in the entire Bible, this word only appears in 1 Timothy 3:2, 1 Timothy 5:7 and 1 Timothy 6:14.[3] When leaders live above reproach, they bring glory to God and keep the focus off themselves and on the gospel.

Why do you think it's important that church leaders live above reproach? How might this apply to all believers as well as church leaders?

Read 1 Peter 5:1-3. How are elders/overseers to *"shepherd the flock"*?

In 1 Timothy 3, most of the qualifications for overseers can be grouped into three categories: family, personal and public.[4] In a way, these characteristics exemplfy how every Christian is called to live, not just leaders. This list could even be seen as ordinary — in one sense, it's simply saying a pastor should be a Christian. The emphasis is on godly character.

Family Characteristics

"The husband of one wife" *(1 Timothy 3:2).*

Effective leader of a household who encourages children to obey *(1 Timothy 3:4).*

Personal Characteristics

"Sober-minded" *(1 Timothy 3:2).*

"Self-controlled" *(1 Timothy 3:2).*

"Not a drunkard" *(1 Timothy 3:3).*

"Not violent but gentle" *(1 Timothy 3:3).*

"Not quarrelsome" *(1 Timothy 3:3).*

"Not a lover of money" *(1 Timothy 3:3).*

Spiritually mature and humble *(1 Timothy 3:6).*

Public Characteristics

"Above reproach" *(1 Timothy 3:2).*

"Respectable" *(1 Timothy 3:2).*

"Hospitable" *(1 Timothy 3:2).*

"Well thought of by outsiders" *(1 Timothy 3:7).*

This list is extensive, and some qualifications seem more straightforward than others. What characteristics stick out to you most, and why?

Look at 1 Timothy 3:4-5 again. Why is it important for an overseer, someone who leads a church, to lead their own household well?

In Paul's list of characteristics, only one is actually based on skill: being *"able to teach"* or instruct church members in the knowledge of God's Word (1 Timothy 3:2). By teaching sound doctrine, elders are to equip the people of God to live out their faith.

How have church leaders helped you understand and apply God's Word to your life?

Church leaders have an enormous responsibility to share and guard the gospel and are on the front lines of spiritual warfare. Take a moment to pray for the leaders in your church or other Christian leaders you know.

Lie that creates chaos:

Personal character is not as important as talent, knowledge or appearance.

Truth that brings clarity:

Humans tend to look at outward appearance when choosing leaders, but God looks at the heart.

TOUGH TOPICS IN 1 TIMOTHY:

What Does the "Husband of One Wife" Mean?

First Timothy 3:2 says an overseer should be *"the husband of one wife,"* but what exactly does that mean? Like with many passages in 1 Timothy, scholars and churches have a range of views on this topic. Here are some brief descriptions of a few views:

1. Some commentators say Paul was teaching that a godly church leader has the "character of a one-woman man" who is faithful in marriage.[1] Though an elder is not *required* to be married in this view, they are required to have the character traits of someone who would be a faithful spouse. Those who hold this view generally do not think the wording is specific enough to be talking about the issues of divorce and remarriage.[2]

2. Some Christians do take *"one wife"* to mean an elder must be married.

3. Related to questions about women serving as elders, some suggest Paul mentioned being a *"husband"* because the role of elder is reserved for qualified men.

4. Others see *"one wife"* as a command prohibiting polygamists from becoming church leaders. Polygamy, or marriage to several spouses at the same time, was a common practice in the Greco-Roman world but is not God's design for marriage (Genesis 2:24).

5. Another theory is that Paul may have been preventing anyone who was married monogamously more than once — whose former spouse was still living — from becoming an elder (see 1 Corinthians 7:39). As a subset of this view, some also include those who remarried after their spouse had died.[3]

Wherever we land in our interpretation of this passage, it's clear that overseers are to set an example for all believers by honoring the covenant of marriage.

WEEK ONE
Weekend Reflection + Prayer

After all we've studied this week … do you feel for Timothy yet? False teachers were purposely distorting the Truth and diluting the gospel in Ephesus. And what was the result of these lies? Chaos, confusion, faithless living and legalism that led to an ineffective church.

Almost 2,000 years later, we can still find ourselves in a mess like this. But praise the Lord that grace is never far away. Like Paul charged Timothy to help the believers around him and to build up the Church by focusing on the gospel and God's love, we are to do the same thing.

But we can't *share the Truth* until we *know the Truth*. Staying connected to Jesus through reading and studying His Word helps train our hearts to discern truth from error. The better we know God's Truth, the faster we will be able to discern when lies come our way.

As we walk this journey, consider praying about who you can invite to walk alongside you in pursuing God's Truth, like how Paul mentored Timothy in the faith. If you are just starting your faith journey, you might ask for God to guide you to a spiritually mature believer who will point you toward Truth, sound teaching and godly character. If you have been walking with Jesus for a while, you might ask that God would send you someone to mentor, someone to whom you can pass on the precious Truth found in the pages of Scripture.

Let's pray.

Dear God, thank You for Your servants Paul and Timothy and their example of a friendship that was rooted in the Truth and work of the gospel. I pray that You would help me keep my eyes firmly fixed on Your Truth and that Your Holy Spirit would help me discern when I'm being deceived by lies. As we move through this study of 1 and 2 Timothy, please increase my understanding and love of Your Word, and help me to share the Truth with the people in my life. In Jesus' name, amen.

NOTES

NOTES

WEEK Two

DAY 6 / 1 TIMOTHY 3:8-13

Paul gave qualifications for those who serve as deacons in the Church.

If you've ever played or watched a team sport, you know every person on the field or court has a specific job to do. A baseball team may have a famous pitcher, but the pitcher can't do his job without a catcher behind home plate. And neither the pitcher nor the catcher can do their jobs without the infielders and outfielders to back them up and make plays.

Like teammates need each other to win a baseball game, the same is true in the Church: Pastors, elders or overseers can't lead all by themselves. Today's scriptures teach us that other servants — specifically, deacons — are also critical to a fully functioning church body. Elders are primarily called to *declare* the gospel through the teaching of the Word of God, and deacons are primarily called to *demonstrate* the gospel through acts of service.[1]

> Overall, the list of qualifications for deacons is similar to the qualifications for overseers. A notable difference is that deacons are not required to teach, though *"they must hold the mystery of the faith with a clear conscience"* (1 Timothy 3:9). Why do you think Paul didn't list teaching as a requirement for deacons?

> In Greek, the word "deacon" is *diakonos*, which means "humble servant."[2] Read Acts 6:1-6 to learn how the role of deacon was instituted in the early Church. Why was it necessary to appoint deacons, and how does this relate to the idea of humble servitude?

The Church is called to love our neighbors (Luke 10:25-28), which includes caring for and serving others, especially those who are suffering, like widows or people experiencing poverty. The role of a deacon within the local church is to take responsibility for leading through serving others, ministering to church members in need and perhaps community members too.

But before a deacon can serve, they are to "*prove themselves blameless*" (1 Timothy 3:10). "*Blameless*" doesn't mean *sinless*, but it does refer to a good reputation. Most scholars agree this means deacons must prove to have godly character over time, demonstrating a lifestyle of service to their church and community before they hold an official leadership position. Some churches reserve the title of deacon for a select few while others expect all church members to be deacons (to lead by example, to be blameless and to serve).

> Deacons are to have a service-minded mentality as an example for all Christians. What is one practical way you can serve your church or community this week?

Regarding the wives of deacons, different churches have various opinions about 1 Timothy 3:11: "*Their wives likewise must be dignified, not slanderers, but sober-minded, faithful in all things.*" The Greek word translated as "*wives*" is *gyne*, which could also just mean "women." Some take the view that Paul was referring to male deacons' wives while others suggest Paul was referring to women serving as deacons or serving as assistants to male deacons. Whatever the case, as an example for all Christian women, these women were called to behave in a Christlike way.

Ultimately, today's scriptures show us the role of a deacon is humble. But there is a spiritual reward in serving well: Deacons have "*good standing*" among fellow Christians and develop "*great confidence in the faith that is in Christ Jesus*" (1 Timothy 3:13). And Colossians 3:23-24 tells **all** believers that if we "*work heartily ... serving the Lord Christ*," then "*from the Lord [we] will receive the inheritance as [our] reward.*"

These are incredible blessings! *The Bible Knowledge Commentary* explains, "Humble service, which lacks all the rewards the world deems important, becomes a true test of one's motives."[3]

> Read Matthew 20:26-28. What did Jesus tell His disciples about servanthood? How does that change the way we live?

> Service can also be an effective method of evangelism. How can acts of service open the door for you to share your faith with others?

While service roles are often behind the scenes, they are critical in the Church. The Church can never have too many members who devote themselves to service. Let's consider how God is leading us to serve today.

Lie that creates chaos:
It is better to be served than to serve others.

Truth that brings clarity:
Believers who serve others may not get recognition from the world, but God is pleased with their humble service in His name.

DAY 7 / 1 TIMOTHY 3:14-16

Paul stated his central purpose for writing to Timothy.

Today's reading is significant because Paul stated his reason for writing to Timothy, and he also gave incredible illustrations of the Church and its purpose – to declare the saving work of Jesus Christ.

Fill in the blanks of 1 Timothy 3:14-15 to discover Paul's purpose in writing:

"I hope to come to you soon, but I am writing these things to you so that, if I delay, you may know how one ought to _____ in the _____ of God, which is the _____ of the living God, a _____ and _____ of the _____."

Paul wanted the Ephesians to know how to conduct themselves in their local church, which helps us understand why he went into detail about qualifications for church leadership and structure.

What are some reasons why you think it's important that Christians know how to behave in church? (One way to answer this is to imagine if there were **no** organized practices or expectations at all about behavior at church … What would be the result?)

In 1 Timothy 3:15, we learn the Church is God's household. This means it's a place where God Himself makes the rules. When loving parents make house rules, they do it for the betterment and protection of their children – and when the children obey those rules, the family functions well. Likewise, our Father wants His children to obey His rules for our own benefit and His glory.[1]

It is a privilege to be called the children of God (1 John 3:1). How does it make you feel to know that the Church is like a household for God's family? How does this shape or change the way you think about the Church?

In the garden of Eden, God walked closely with Adam and Eve – but then humanity's sin broke our relationship with God (Genesis 3). Still, He created other ways to be with His people. First God dwelled in a movable worship structure called the tabernacle, and later He dwelled in a more permanent temple in the midst of His people in Israel. Yet even at the temple, sinful people could not enter directly into God's presence. Only priests could do so on special occasions, after performing purification rituals (Hebrews 9:2-7).

But because of Jesus' sacrifice on the cross, the Holy Spirit dwells within believers today — we ourselves are "*the temple of the living God*" (2 Corinthians 6:16)! And when people indwelled by the Holy Spirit gather as the Church, it is a holy and special occasion.[2]

Read Ephesians 2:19-22. What are God's people being "*built together into*"?

First Timothy 3:15 also says the Church is a pillar and buttress of Truth. In architecture, buttresses and pillars uphold a structure. The Church has the important assignment of upholding the Truth of God's Word, preserving it from false teachers, and proclaiming it to the world. This is the primary responsibility of believers in local churches. The word "church" comes from the Greek word *ekklesia*, which literally means "gathering" or "assembly," and refers to the weekly worship gathering of God's people. While parachurch organizations, like nonprofits or other ministries, can be effective and Spirit-filled, Jesus Himself said, "*I will build my **church**, and the gates of hell shall not prevail against it*" (Matthew 16:18, emphasis added).

Finally, 1 Timothy 3:16 says the Church confesses "*the mystery of godliness*," and many scholars suggest that what follows is a first-century hymn. This short song succinctly declares the supremacy of Christ. The way to salvation was once mysterious, but Jesus solved this mystery since He is the embodiment of godliness. Friend, Jesus has also given us everything *we* need for godliness (2 Peter 1:3)!

What do you think it means to be godly in Christ? As we close today's study, thank Him for revealing the mystery of godliness to you.

Lie that creates chaos:

The local church is just an old-fashioned institution.

Truth that brings clarity:

The Church has a unique role in God's plan to bring salvation to the world, and believers in Christ are called to actively participate in local gatherings.

THE GOSPEL IN A FIRST-CENTURY HYMN

Many scholars believe 1 Timothy 3:16 was a first-century hymn written to declare the gospel. This is God's plan of salvation for the world!

1 Timothy 3:16	*Theological Interpretation*
"He was manifested in the flesh"	This describes the incarnation of Jesus, who came to earth to live as a human while remaining fully God. ("Incarnation" literally means "in the flesh.")
"vindicated by the Spirit"	Some scholars see this as a description of Jesus' resurrection since Jesus was vindicated (justified, freed, declared righteous) before heavenly beings when He rose from the dead.[1] (See Romans 1:4.)
"seen by angels"	This could possibly refer to Jesus' ascension back to heaven after His resurrection.
"proclaimed among the nations"	Jesus preached the gospel to all people, and so do we.
"believed on in the world"	Jesus' message is effective, and many have received and will receive salvation by faith in Him.
"taken up in glory"	Some scholars also see this line as referring to the ascension of Jesus into heaven. Others see this as a reference to the glorious second coming of Christ.

DAY 8 / 1 TIMOTHY 4:1-5

Paul said some people will walk away from the faith.

If you live in an area with inclement weather, you probably know the importance of storm warnings. These warnings give people time to prepare and take cover so they aren't caught off guard by the storm.

Today's scriptures show us that Paul didn't want Timothy or the church at Ephesus to be caught off guard by the fact that *"in later times some will depart from the faith by devoting themselves to deceitful spirits and teachings of demons"* (1 Timothy 4:1). Paul didn't give this warning to stir up self-doubt or fear in the hearts of believers, but he wanted them to see true faith as an active walk with Christ — not just a one-time commitment but an enduring relationship.

> Have you ever known a leader, friend or church member who walked away from faith in Jesus? How did that impact your own faith?

> In John 15:4-5, Jesus said, *"Abide in me, and I in you … for apart from me you can do nothing."* What do you think abiding looks like, and how does it protect us against *"depart[ing] from the faith"* (1 Timothy 4:1)?

First Timothy 4:1 is the only place where demons are mentioned in 1 and 2 Timothy. This reminds us that Satan not only works to deceive people outside the Church but within the Church through *"liars"* (v. 2) who attempt to lead God's people astray. The consciences of these false teachers are *"seared"* (v. 2), meaning they are spiritually desensitized to what they are doing. As we defend our churches and ourselves against false teaching, we can remember what Paul said in Ephesians 6:12: *"For we do not wrestle against flesh and blood, but against the rulers, against the authorities, against the cosmic powers over this present darkness, against the spiritual forces of evil in the heavenly places."*

> Read Matthew 7:15-20. How does Jesus describe false teachers, and how does He say we will recognize them?

What did the false teachers "*forbid*" and "*require*" in 1 Timothy 4:3? Why do you think this is significant?

We don't know the background of what led to these prohibitions, but it seems Paul was addressing ascetic teachings, which were based on the belief that self-denial contributed to a person's salvation. This runs contrary to the gospel Truth that we cannot earn our salvation. So Paul confronted asceticism with the truth that food and marriage are created by God. Even though humans can commit sins related to food (for example, gluttony) or sins in the context of marriage (for example, sexual immorality or abusive behavior), neither marriage nor food is evil in and of itself. "*For everything created by God is good …*" (1 Timothy 4:4).

Pastor and Bible teacher David Platt observes that false teachers make two common errors: They deny God's goodness and distort His Word.[1] People who walk away from the faith often do so because they come to believe one or both of these lies.

Friend, the battle for souls is real, and the stakes are life and death. Thankfully we can speak the name of Jesus over the lies — He is the Truth!

Read Acts 20:28-32. After warning about false teachers, what did Paul say God is "*able to build*" and "*give*" in verse 32? How does this encourage you to keep the faith?

Lie that creates chaos:

There is nothing spiritual about false teaching; people are just misinformed or have different opinions.

Truth that brings clarity:

Purposeful distortion of the Word of God is a tactic of Satan to confuse those inside and outside the Church.

TOUGH TOPICS IN 1 TIMOTHY:

Can Christians Lose Their Salvation?

First Timothy 1:19 says, "*Some have made shipwreck of their faith.*" What exactly could this mean?

The short answer to the question of whether or not a person can lose their salvation is that it depends on who you ask: Some would say apostates do lose their salvation while others would say true believers simply won't. "Apostasy" means denying or turning from one's faith after previously claiming to trust in Christ.

Believers across history have developed different viewpoints on this issue based on their study of Scripture. Two of the most famous and distinct perspectives come from theologians John Calvin and Jacob Arminius, but the discussion is as ancient as Scripture itself, also including debates between Augustine and Pelagius, Luther and Erasmus, and others. Two theological keywords that distinguish each side are "monergism" and "synergism." "Monergism" literally means "one working" while "synergism" means "together working."

Those who align with a more monergist view of salvation suggest that when God saves a person through faith in His Son, their salvation can never be lost because He is the One who secures it. Those who agree with a more synergist view tend to maintain that just as each believer chooses to trust in Christ of their own volition, some believers later choose to reject Christ, therefore losing their salvation. This is how synergist theology would account for apostasy.

A more monergistic explanation of apostasy might say that people who permanently walk away from the faith never truly placed their faith in Jesus (1 John 2:19). In this view, apostasy is different from a believer experiencing a *temporary* time of rebellion but later returning to Christ (without losing their salvation in the meantime).

Whatever our personal convictions about this topic may be, in the end, we can all praise God that those who are truly in Christ and remain in Christ will be eternally reconciled to God!

Let's conclude with just a couple of scriptures that help us appreciate the tensions and truths we are to hold together:

Regarding the permanence, safety and security of our salvation ...

In John 6:39-40, Jesus says, *"And this is the will of him who sent me, that I should lose nothing of all that he has given me, but raise it up on the last day. For this is the will of my Father, that everyone who looks on the Son and believes in him should have eternal life, and I will raise him up on the last day."*

In John 10:27-29, Jesus says, *"My sheep hear my voice, and I know them, and they follow me. I give them eternal life, and they will never perish, and no one will snatch them out of my hand. My Father, who has given them to me, is greater than all, and no one is able to snatch them out of the Father's hand."*

Regarding the ongoing preservation of our salvation through faith ...

Ephesians 1:13-14 says, *"In [Christ] you also, when you heard the word of truth, the gospel of your salvation, and believed in him, were sealed with the promised Holy Spirit, who is the guarantee of our inheritance until we acquire possession of it, to the praise of his glory."*

Hebrews 3:14 says, *"For we have come to share in Christ, if indeed we hold our original confidence firm to the end."* (See also Hebrews 6:4-6).

DAY 9 / 1 TIMOTHY 4:6-16

Paul encouraged Timothy to train himself for godliness.

Elite athletes dedicate hours to training each week to get their bodies into peak condition for competition. When they persevere in training, they see positive results. In today's reading, we learn that the path to becoming Christlike is like an athlete's path to becoming physically fit — we need to be disciplined to see growth.

Paul encouraged Timothy to put his training in faith and "*good doctrine*" into practice by declaring God's Truth to the Church and avoiding "*irreverent, silly myths*" (1 Timothy 4:6-7). He wanted Timothy not to waste his time with distractions but to devote himself to spiritual training instead.

> We are all surrounded by distractions that keep us from pursuing godliness. What are some distractions in your life, and how can you resist them to remain focused on Christ?

The Greek word for "*train*" in 1 Timothy 4:6-7 is *gymnaze*, which is where we get our English word "gymnastic." In the ancient world, this referred to bodily training of any kind. But while physical fitness is a worthy goal, Paul said training for "*godliness is of value in every way, as it holds promise for the present life and also for the life to come*" (1 Timothy 4:8). Paul wasn't diminishing physical fitness, but he was putting it in its proper place. Spiritual fitness impacts eternity.

With this in mind, in 1 Timothy 4:11-16, Paul then gave specific direction to Timothy about his spiritual role as a pastor. Some may have questioned Timothy's pastoral authority because of his age; most commentators estimate he was in his late 20s to mid 30s.[1] But Paul challenged him to build his credibility by demonstrating godliness in five specific areas.

> What were these five areas of godliness in 1 Timothy 4:12? List them below. What would it look like to set an example in these areas?

Next, Paul gave Timothy three elements of effective preaching in 1 Timothy 4:13, which also serve as an example for all of us as Christians:

1. *"Public reading of Scripture."*
2. *"Exhortation,"* or urging others to obey the Lord.
3. *"Teaching."*

Why do you think *"keep[ing] a close watch on [himself] and on the teaching"* (v. 16) was so critical for Timothy and the church in Ephesus, and why is it still critical for the Church today?

As an overseer of pastors, Timothy was in a spiritual battle for the hearts and minds of the people in Ephesus. Paul didn't want him to neglect his spiritual gift and calling to teach the Truth found in God's Word. Like all of us, Timothy needed to be disciplined to *"practice"* his spiritual gifts (1 Timothy 4:15). Spiritual gifts are given by the indwelling Holy Spirit, but our responsibility is to refine and improve our exercising of these gifts to build up the Church (1 Corinthians 14:12). For example, someone called to teach the Bible is to keep studying and learning, taking the time to prepare and craft messages that communicate God's Truth clearly.

You can read more about spiritual gifts in 1 Corinthians 12-14 and Romans 12:6-8. What spiritual gift(s) is God calling you to cultivate for His glory? What practical steps can you take to grow in this area of godliness?

Whether or not you work in vocational ministry like Timothy, if you are in Christ, God has specifically called you to urge others to love and obey Him for the glory of His Kingdom. Devote yourself to the Truth found in His Word, and trust Him with the results!

Lie that creates chaos:

People don't need to be disciplined to be godly.

Truth that brings clarity:

Cultivating godliness takes effort and discipline. Devoting ourselves to reading and understanding the Bible, praying, and maintaining accountability with other believers produces godly character over time.

DAY 10 / 1 TIMOTHY 5:1-16

Paul instructed the Church on how to care for each other as God's family.

Worldwide, there are an estimated 258 million widows, and one in 10 widows lives in poverty.[1] With numbers this high, chances are that you know a widow, are a widow, or have a widow in your family. In today's passage, we learn how the family of God is meant to care for and honor one another, especially those who are vulnerable, like widows.

Read 1 Timothy 5:1-2. How did Paul tell Timothy to treat these four groups of people?

OLDER MEN:

YOUNGER MEN:

OLDER WOMEN:

YOUNGER WOMEN:

All Christ followers are to treat older men and women in the Church with respect, like we would treat our own parents. Younger men and women are to be treated as brothers and sisters — because in Christ, we're all children of the Father. First Timothy 5:2 also prompts us to encourage one another *"in all purity,"* just as Paul earlier instructed Timothy to *"set the believers an example in speech, in conduct, in love, in faith, in purity"* (1 Timothy 4:12).

How does thinking of fellow believers as your family shape the way you interact with them? What does it look like for believers to be pure in our relationships with one another?

"Honor" is another key word in today's passage, meaning "to hold someone in high regard." First Timothy 5:3 says widows are to be esteemed in the household of God — which is often the opposite of how they are viewed in the world. In Paul's first-century context, wives relied on their husbands for both social standing and a steady income, so unmarried widows were often resigned to a life of poverty. Some saw widows as a burden on their community. But thank God, His love is not defined by what the world sees! God's economy is upside down: He *"opposes the proud but gives grace to the humble"* (James 4:6; 1 Peter 5:5).

James 1:27 says, "*Religion that is pure and undefiled before God the Father is this: to visit orphans and widows in their affliction, and to keep oneself unstained from the world.*" Why is caring for widows and others in need an expression of true faith in Christ?

Paul pointed out that caring for a widow is first her family's responsibility. What do 1 Timothy 5:4 and verse 8 say about providing for relatives?

Scholars believe the church in Ephesus was experiencing financial strain because some were refusing to provide for their widowed family members. That's likely why Paul gave specific instructions about not only honoring widows but giving monetary support. For a godly widow who was *"left all alone"* with no one to support her, Paul told the Church to offer help (v. 5).

John Koessler says, "A true widow in the biblical sense is marked by both genuine need and godly character."[2] Verse 5 gives an important clue as to the source of a faithful widow's strength: She "*has set her hope on God and continues in supplications and prayers night and day.*"

How can devotion to prayer help you through hardships in your own life?

Finally, widows younger than 60 were not to receive financial assistance from the Church; Paul advised them to remarry, have children, and devote themselves to family life (1 Timothy 5:14). Yet Paul also said a widow's *"desire to marry"* could *"draw them away from Christ"* (vv. 11–12). Was he recommending remarriage or not?

A little more context can provide clarity: Scholars suggest that verses 11–12 were directed toward "some young widows [who] pledged to serve the church as widows in exchange for a stipend," but their *true desire* was to marry. Eventually, "lacking the gift of singleness, [they] were finally overcome and wed the first man who came along," even if he didn't follow Jesus.[3] Paul urged such widows to seek godly husbands in the Church instead.

What were some temptations for younger widows with too much time on their hands (1 Timothy 5:13)? How can you resist these temptations whether you're married or not?

As we close today's study, let's ask God to show us how we can show special honor to a widow or another person in need this week.

Lie that creates chaos:
Widows have nothing to offer the local church.

Truth that brings clarity:
Widows are dearly loved by God and indispensable to the local church; they can provide wisdom, kindness and prayer to fellow believers.

WIDOWS IN THE BIBLE

Widows hold a special place in the biblical narrative, often exemplifying faith, courage and the mercy of God. In the Old Testament, God made provisions to protect the widows among His people (Exodus 22:22; Isaiah 1:16-17), and in the New Testament, Jesus also cared for widows in particular (Mark 12:38-40; Luke 7:11-17).[1]

Although this chart doesn't contain an exhaustive list of widows in the Bible, it helps us see God's heart for women who may feel alone in the world. God is a *"protector of widows"* (Psalm 68:5), and they will always have a special place in His family.

Widow	What She's Known For	Where To Find Her
TAMAR	Tamar was widowed twice in Genesis 38. She engaged in a form of sexual sin, but God ultimately redeemed her story. She became the mother of Perez and Zerah, sons of Judah, and is one of the women listed in the lineage of Jesus.	Genesis 38; Matthew 1:3
ABIGAIL	Originally the wife of Nabal, Abigail *"was discerning and beautiful"* (1 Samuel 25:3). She prevented King David from carrying out a rash plan to kill her foolish husband, who did not allow the king to have food and shelter. In the end, God took Nabal's life as a just consequence for his sins. Not long after, David married wise Abigail.	1 Samuel 25
NAOMI AND RUTH	Naomi and Ruth were a mother- and daughter-in-law who found themselves widowed at the same time. God redeemed both of their stories by sending Boaz to marry Ruth, who later gave birth to Obed. From Ruth's family line came King David and eventually Jesus. Ruth is one of five women included in Jesus' genealogy.	Ruth 1-4; Matthew 1:5

Widow	What She's Known For	Where To Find Her
THE WIDOW AT ZAREPHATH	She fed the prophet Elijah with her small amount of oil and flour, and miraculously, the oil and flour never ran out. When her son died shortly thereafter, God raised him back to life.	1 Kings 17:8-24
THE WIDOW ELISHA HELPED	This widow needed to pay her debts, and the prophet Elisha instructed her to get jars to fill with oil. Miraculously, all the jars were filled, and the widow was able to sell the oil to pay her debts and live on the remaining money.	2 Kings 4:1-7
ANNA	Anna was a prophetess and widow who prayed day and night at the temple for the coming of the Messiah. When she met Jesus in the temple on the day of His dedication, she gave thanks to the Lord.	Luke 2:36-38
THE WIDOW WITH TWO COINS	Jesus commended her for her generous heart. Though she was poor, she gave *"all she had to live on"* to support the Lord's work at the temple (Mark 12:44).	Mark 12:41-44; Luke 21:1-4
THE WIDOW AT NAIN	Jesus raised this widow's only son from the dead.	Luke 7:11-17

WEEK TWO
Weekend Reflection + Prayer

This week's readings remind us that while sound doctrine is the foundation of our faith, good theology goes beyond "head knowledge" – it transforms our hearts to live in obedience to God, in service to the Church, and in compassionate care for the vulnerable.

When we take God's Truth and apply it to the way we live, the result will be godliness. The more we know Jesus, the more we will love Him, and the more we love Jesus, the more we will become like Him. Like the Apostle James said, "*Faith by itself, if it does not have works, is dead*" (James 2:17). We can't earn salvation through our own works; it is a free gift of grace we receive when we trust in Christ. But for all who do receive this gift, faith that is alive and vibrant will express itself not only in our confession of the gospel but in how we live it out.

How do we solve the "*mystery*" of what it means to live godly lives (1 Timothy 3:16)? We look to Jesus, who set the perfect example. He saw our need and "*emptied himself, by taking the form of a servant, being born in the likeness of men. And being found in human form, he humbled himself by becoming obedient to the point of death, even death on a cross*" (Philippians 2:7-8).

Jesus' sacrifice sets believers free from the bondage of sin and ungodliness. The Holy Spirit dwells within all who confess Jesus as Lord and helps us to live grateful lives of obedience to the Father. As Paul said, "*Godliness is of value in every way, as it holds promise for the present life and also for the life to come*" (1 Timothy 4:8).

Let's pray.

Dear God, thank You for giving me everything I need for "life and godliness" (2 Peter 1:3). I pray that my life would reflect You and bear the fruit of the Spirit (Galatians 5:22-23). Help me to be part of building up the body of Christ through my local church and to share the gospel through the testimony of my words and actions. Most of all, thank You for Jesus, who has set my heart free with His redeeming sacrifice of love and His victorious resurrection. I pray that I never get over Your abundant grace and mercy. In Jesus' name, amen.

NOTES

NOTES

WEEK Three

DAY 11 / 1 TIMOTHY 5:17-25
Paul gave instructions regarding care for church elders.

Last week, we started studying what it means to care for one another in the family of God, looking at widows first. Today, we'll take a closer look at what it means to honor church leaders who have committed their lives to serving the people of God.

Church members and pastors are to mutually serve one another in a healthy church body. And Paul told Timothy that "*elders who rule well*" are "*worthy of double honor, especially those who labor in preaching and teaching*" (1 Timothy 5:17). The word "*labor*" is *kopiao* in Greek and can also be translated as "toil," which "implies hard work that makes a person tired."[1] Preaching and teaching is hard work!

In light of this, "*double honor*" does not necessarily mean pastors should be paid double, but it does imply they should be compensated generously, if possible, by their church family and be treated with respect. First Timothy 5:18 refers to a law in Deuteronomy 25:4 that prohibited muzzling a working ox — because the ox should eat the grain it works hard to grind. Similarly, churches should not withhold provisions from their hardworking pastors. Paul also quoted Jesus, who said, "*The laborer deserves his wages*" (Luke 10:7).[2]

> How does providing generous compensation to pastors show them honor? What might differentiate generous compensation from undercompensation or overcompensation?

Paul also addressed the problem of accusations against church elders, requiring two or three witnesses to bring a complaint (1 Timothy 5:19). Due to the public nature of their jobs, pastors are very susceptible to criticism and even slander. And it's not simply the physical, mental or social work of being a pastor that can be difficult: If we consider that all believers are engaged in spiritual battle, then leaders in such battles must face especially great opposition (Ephesians 6:12).

Because their roles are so important, Paul is clear that allegations of leaders' misconduct are to be taken seriously and that churches should make every effort to bring the truth into the light. Church elders aren't perfect people; they sometimes sin just like all of us do. But Paul distinguished that elders who "*persist in sin*," continuing a pattern of habitual sin and refusing to repent, are to be publicly corrected (1 Timothy 5:20). As we've already learned, this discipline is motivated by love, intended to lead to repentance (1 Timothy 1:5).

> What are some possible consequences of accusing someone of a sin they didn't commit? How might this explain Paul's instruction to investigate allegations thoroughly (v. 19)?

Read James 3:1. Based on this verse, why is it important for leaders to be held accountable?

Perhaps you've been personally hurt by a church leader's sin. Friend, if so, please know that it breaks God's heart when these things occur in His family. How does today's reading give you comfort that God takes sin and justice seriously?

Paul also wanted Timothy to proceed with caution when appointing elders: "*Do not be hasty in the laying on of hands, nor take part in the sins of others; keep yourself pure*" (1 Timothy 5:22). Being too quick to appoint an elder may result in the appointment of someone who is unfit to serve. A person may appear like a good fit but have a hidden pattern of sin that "*appear[s] later*" (v. 24). David Platt says, "The main point here is that we need to take all the time, care, and due diligence necessary to make sure [an elder] is qualified to the best of our knowledge."[3]

What are some reasons why it's important to take the time to appoint qualified church leaders?

Knowing that pastors and elders work hard to deliver God's Truth and shepherd His people, what is one way you can honor your pastor or another Christian leader who has positively impacted your life?

Lie that creates chaos:
Ministry leadership is an easy job.

Truth that brings clarity:
Church leaders are to work tirelessly to declare God's Truth, care for His people, and maintain a high level of personal integrity.

TOUGH TOPICS IN 1 TIMOTHY:

Why Did Paul Tell Timothy To Drink Wine?

A verse that has puzzled many Christians is 1 Timothy 5:23: *"(No longer drink only water, but use a little wine for the sake of your stomach and your frequent ailments.)"*

While this verse may seem out of place, it likely refers back to the phrase that comes before it: *"Keep yourself pure"* (1 Timothy 5:22). In Ephesus, false teachers preached different forms of asceticism (extreme abstaining from anything considered worldly) that may have included encouraging church members to drink only water. Yet 1 Timothy 4:3-5 warns against those who *"require abstinence from foods that God created to be received with thanksgiving by those who believe and know the truth. For everything created by God is good, and nothing is to be rejected if it is received with thanksgiving, for it is made holy by the word of God and prayer."* Many commentators believe that in these verses, Paul was putting Timothy's mind at ease about drinking a temperate amount of wine for his stomach issues, as this would not compromise his spiritual purity.

It's common to hear that wine in the Bible was more like grape juice, but this is actually not accurate. The *Baker Encyclopedia of the Bible* explains:

> "... In the [Old Testament], wine was used without being mixed with water. The terminology of mixing water and wine is strikingly unattested. Wine diluted with water was symbolic of spiritual adulteration (Isaiah 1:22). By Roman times this attitude changed ... [but] a natural, nondistilled wine could reach as high as 15 percent alcohol content. If watered down 3 parts water to 1 part wine, the alcohol content would be 5 percent and still fairly potent."[1]

Also notable about wine in the ancient world is that the cleanliness of water in places like Ephesus was probably hit or miss. Today many people have access to reliable water filtration systems, but in Ephesus, most likely it was safer to drink wine than water on many occasions. As 1 Timothy 5:23 says, wine had some health benefits. Still, the Bible does warn against drunkenness and overconsumption of alcohol (e.g., Ephesians 5:18; Proverbs 23:29-35).

With all this in mind, there are also many good and biblical reasons why an individual might choose to abstain from alcohol completely. Our role as believers is to follow the Holy Spirit's conviction in our own hearts, not to pass judgment on others who abstain or who don't. Romans 14:21-23 summarizes, *"It is good not to eat meat or drink wine or do anything that causes your brother to stumble. The faith that you have, keep between yourself and God. Blessed is the one who has no reason to pass judgment on himself for what he approves. But whoever has doubts is condemned if he eats, because the eating is not from faith. For whatever does not proceed from faith is sin."*

Today we can understand Paul's words to Timothy not as an encouragement to drink alcohol however we please but as a reminder that both our spiritual and physical health are important to God. For some, complete abstinence from alcohol truly is best. For everyone, anything we use improperly or excessively can be unhealthy — but as we grow in godliness, we learn to practice wisdom and to care for our bodies as temples of the Holy Spirit (1 Corinthians 6:19-20).

DAY 12 / 1 TIMOTHY 6:1-10

Paul taught that godliness leads to contentment and great gain.

Have you ever heard someone say, "He's such a poser"? "Poser" is a slang term for someone who pretends to be something they are not. And in today's reading, Paul called out posers in Ephesus. He warned against people doing things in the name of Christianity but actually serving their own purposes, seeking fame, accolades or wealth.

After Paul addressed "*bondservants*" honoring their masters (see Page 65 for more on 1 Timothy 6:1-2), he didn't waste time in calling out the posers, exposing false Christians by comparing them to true Christians.

> According to 1 Timothy 6:3-4, what does a person who "*teaches a different doctrine and does not agree with the sound words of our Lord Jesus Christ*" have an "*unhealthy craving*" for? What do those cravings produce?

These teachers' minds were corrupted and deceived (2 Timothy 3:8), and they saw godliness as "*a means of gain*" (1 Timothy 6:5). They were motivated by greed, perhaps seeing ministry as a way to financial prosperity. Even though pastors can be paid for their service to the Church, accumulation of financial wealth is not the right motivation for a life in ministry.

> Greed is not just a moral issue — it's a spiritual battle. First Timothy 6:10 says, "*For the love of money is a root of all kinds of evils.*" Money isn't intrinsically evil, but the human heart can evilly make money a priority over God. How do you battle against greed in your own heart?

> There's good news! Fill in the blanks of 1 Timothy 6:6:
>
> "But _____ with _____ is great _____."

When we seek God not for what we can get out of Him but for the sheer joy of knowing Him, we will find the very thing we long for — true contentment. Jesus holds the answer to our hearts' deepest longings. False teachers may indicate that godliness always leads to worldly success, but the truth is that believers are "*rich in faith*" (James 2:5) even if, in a worldly sense, we have only our basic needs met (1 Timothy 6:8). We can be satisfied in Christ.

Paul, while imprisoned, said in Philippians 4:11-13, "*I have learned in whatever situation I am to be content. I know how to be brought low, and I know how to abound. In any and every circumstance, I have learned the secret of facing plenty and hunger, abundance and need. I can do all things through him who strengthens me.*" What does it look like for you to be content in every situation?

Read Matthew 6:19-21. What does it mean to store up "*treasures in heaven*" (v. 20)?

In what areas of your life might God be asking you to be content with Him and what He has given you? As we close today's study, consider writing 1 Timothy 6:6 on a notecard or sticky note and placing it in an easily visible place to remind you that godliness and contentment go hand in hand.

Lie that creates chaos:
Godliness will always bring us material wealth, health and success.

Truth that brings clarity:
True godliness produces contentment through a relationship with Jesus — He is all we need!

TOUGH TOPICS IN 1 TIMOTHY:

Why Does Paul Talk About Slavery?

Although some have misused passages like 1 Timothy 6:1-2 to claim that slavery is acceptable in God's eyes, that's not what Paul was saying in this passage about "*bondservants regard[ing] their own masters.*"

First, we know all forms of slavery are a consequence of human sin and brokenness in our world. Because of sin, the world God designed for our joy and His glory is "*subjected to futility,*" and "*creation itself ... [is in] bondage to corruption*" (Romans 8:20-21). Yet God reaches into our broken world with justice and mercy. One example of this mercy is how God gave rules in the Old Testament to protect and provide for slaves or servants, outlawing physical abuse and mistreatment (Leviticus 25; Exodus 21:16; Exodus 21:26-27).

Furthermore, it may be helpful to understand that the Greek word *doulos* (translated as "*bondservant*" in 1 Timothy 6) "refer[s] to ancient practices and institutions that do not correspond directly to those in the modern world." According to the *ESV Study Bible*, in the New Testament, a *doulos* was someone who was contractually "bound to serve his master for a specific (usually lengthy) period of time, but also someone who might nevertheless own property, achieve social advancement, and even be released or purchase his freedom."[1]

Some scholars estimate that slaves or bondservants made up one-third of the general population in Paul's time, so this impacted everyone in some way.[2] In 1 Timothy 6:1-2, Paul was speaking to some believers who happened to be bondservants and others who happened to be masters, but his main goal was not to make a point about socioeconomic systems of servitude. His point was that no matter who you were, there were expectations of how to *behave in the household of God* (1 Timothy 3:15).

Whether their masters were unbelievers or believers, bondservants were to obey authority for the sake of the gospel. And Paul taught that this obedience was **not** based on bondservants being inferior, for *"there is neither Jew nor Greek, there is neither slave nor free, there is no male and female, for you are all one in Christ Jesus"* (Galatians 3:28). Instead, Paul was encouraging bondservants to work hard, especially for believing masters, precisely because they were "*brothers*" in God's family (1 Timothy 6:2).

In Colossians 4:1, Paul also said, "*Masters, treat your bondservants justly and fairly, knowing that you also have a Master in heaven.*" Both bondservants and masters were equally loved and valued by God, and all were responsible to Him for their own behavior.

Let's remember today that God has called all of us to bear witness to His grace in our lives and to serve others humbly in Jesus' name (Matthew 20:28; Matthew 23:11). And let's also remember that Jesus Christ came to free all believers from slavery to sin — so wherever the gospel goes, freedom goes too.

DAY 13 / 1 TIMOTHY 6:11-21

Paul closed his first letter to Timothy with a reminder to fight the good fight of faith.

In soccer, the goalie's job is to keep the ball out of the net. To prevent the other team from scoring, a good goalie will jump, throw their body on the ground, or do whatever it takes to guard the goal.

Today's reading gives a similar message about guarding the gospel — we are to do whatever it takes to prevent lies from corrupting the Truth. But unlike a soccer game, where the stakes are relatively low, this is a battle for the eternal destinies of people. Thankfully victory doesn't ultimately depend on our performance: Jesus has already won through His life, death and resurrection! We get to be on His team, fighting for His Truth.

At the beginning of this letter, Paul told Timothy to "*wage the good warfare*" (1 Timothy 1:18). Today we conclude the book of 1 Timothy with Paul's final instructions: "*Fight the good fight of the faith*" (1 Timothy 6:12a). For Timothy to successfully complete his mission for Christ, he needed to recognize the spiritual battle at hand. And we, too, have a spiritual enemy who wants to "defame God's glory, distort the gospel, and destroy God's people."[1]

> How does knowing that faith is a daily battle help you prioritize your relationship with God? What does fighting for your faith look like?

Paul instructed Timothy to "*pursue righteousness, godliness, faith, love, steadfastness, gentleness*" (1 Timothy 6:11b). Some scholars compare these character traits to the fruit of the Spirit in Galatians 5:22-23, freely given to every believer in Jesus Christ. But that's not to say these are automatic qualities; cultivating godliness takes work on our part as we yield to the Holy Spirit's work in and through us (1 Corinthians 3:7).

> In your own life, what might you need to "*flee*," and what might you need to actively "*pursue*," to cultivate godliness (1 Timothy 6:11)?

Scholars have different opinions about what "*commandment*" Timothy was supposed to keep in 1 Timothy 6:14. Some believe Paul was referencing all he had instructed Timothy to do throughout his letter, others believe "*commandment*" referred to Timothy's initial call to ministry, and others think it referred to the immediate context of purity in character.[2] In any case, we know Jesus Himself says, "*If you love me, you will keep my commandments*" (John 14:15), meaning God's Word as a whole.

In 1 Timothy 6:15-16, Paul couldn't help but praise Jesus, and he made three statements about His character that remind us why He's worthy of our obedience:

1. He is "*Sovereign.*"
2. He is "*the King of kings and Lord of lords.*"
3. He is immortal and "*dwells in unapproachable light.*"

What do these statements tell us about the greatness of God? What other aspects of God's character motivate you to obey Him?

Finally, Paul gave rich members of the Church instructions on how to properly handle money and material blessings in 1 Timothy 6:17-19.

How do these instructions also apply to all Christians, regardless of economic status?

One last reminder was necessary: "*Guard the deposit entrusted to you*" (1 Timothy 6:20a). Timothy was entrusted with the gospel, the precious message of Jesus' life, death and resurrection. But the church in Ephesus was under spiritual attack. To preserve the gospel there, Timothy had to remain steadfast.

Every generation of the Church has this same charge to preserve and hold up the gospel – to stand for Truth, remain faithful to God's Word, and share the grace of Jesus. Not only do we need to guard Truth in the local church but in our homes and friend groups.

If that sounds overwhelming ... it would be if we had to do it ourselves! But we do not fight this battle alone. The Holy Spirit empowers us.

How is God leading you to "*guard the deposit*" of the gospel in your life (1 Timothy 6:20a)? As we close the book of 1 Timothy, consider praying about how you can take what you've learned and build up your local church and community with truth, humility and love.

Lie that creates chaos:

You only need to guard the gospel if you work in church ministry.

Truth that brings clarity:

Every Christian is called to guard the gospel and stand up for the Truth of God's Word.

Welcome to
2 TIMOTHY

DAY 14 / 2 TIMOTHY 1:1-7

Paul asserted that the Holy Spirit gives love, power and self-control to followers of Christ.

We've all been there — discouraged, tired, and feeling like we just don't have what it takes to answer the call God has placed on our lives. Timothy, like all of us, apparently needed encouragement to use the gifts God had given him. That's why Paul sent his second letter with the words Timothy needed to hear.

Paul probably wrote 2 Timothy from a Roman prison cell, as he had been arrested on his fourth missionary journey. This was likely Paul's last imprisonment before he was put to death. It is important to remember this as we read because much of this letter can be understood as a farewell to his "*beloved child*" Timothy (2 Timothy 1:2).

Paul said he "*constantly*" prayed for Timothy (v. 3), something he would have been able to devote more time to in prison. And his prayers were effective. While these letters from Paul have since resounded across the globe, at the time, Paul couldn't verbally declare the gospel outside the prison walls. But Timothy could — and Paul knew his prayers impacted this work.

> Why do you think Paul devoted so much of his time to praying for Timothy specifically? How could you follow Paul's example by faithfully praying for others even while you wait for God to move in your own hard situation?

Some scholars believe the "*tears*" Paul referenced in verse 4 were from the last time Timothy had seen Paul, which may have been on the day of his arrest.[1] Yet Paul was also "*filled with joy*" (v. 4) because of Timothy's loyalty and "*sincere faith*," a spiritual heritage passed down by two prominent women in Timothy's life: his mother and grandmother (v. 5).

> Think about your spiritual heritage. This may include biological relatives but could also include spiritual "parents," friends or mentors, like Paul was to Timothy. How have other Christians encouraged, taught, discipled and shared their faith with you?

Likewise, who are you sharing your faith with, or how could you help someone else grow closer to Jesus?

Timothy not only preached the gospel, but he lived it out. Paul knew this sincere faith could have a huge impact for the sake of the gospel, so he urged Timothy to "*fan into flame the gift of God*" (2 Timothy 1:6), meaning Timothy's ministry and spiritual gifts.

Why do you think Paul used the metaphor "*fan into flame*" in verse 6? Read Hebrews 12:28-29 and Acts 2:2-4. How do these verses help us see that God's power can be like a fire?

How is the Holy Spirit challenging you to fan the flame of faith in your own life through this study?

Most Bible commentators believe Timothy struggled with timidity and lack of confidence, which may be why Paul told him, "*God gave us a spirit not of fear but of power and love and self-control*" (2 Timothy 1:7).

THE HOLY SPIRIT GIVES US:

+ **POWER** to overcome our fears and to use our gifts to serve others.
+ Supernatural **LOVE** — the opposite of selfishness — that sacrifices on behalf of others, both fellow believers and those who are lost.
+ **SELF-CONTROL**, which can also be translated as "*self-discipline*" (v. 7, NIV) or "*a sound mind*" (KJV). The Holy Spirit helps us obey God and order our lives and thoughts in a way that's pleasing to Him.

Let's also recognize what God has *not given* us: a spirit of fear. Fear is a liar; it tells us that God isn't good and that He can't or won't supply what we need. But the truth is that we can have courage for today because we know our God holds tomorrow (and yesterday, the distant future, and every moment in between!).

Read 1 John 4:18-19. How does God's perfect love cast out fear in your life?

Lie that creates chaos:
We have no choice but to let our fears control us.

Truth that brings clarity:
Through the indwelling of the Holy Spirit, we can replace fear with power, love and self-control.

DAY 15 / 2 TIMOTHY 1:8-18

Paul told Timothy not to be ashamed of the gospel and to share in his suffering.

Over the course of Church history, devoted followers of Jesus have suffered, and many have died, because they were not ashamed to proclaim their faith boldly. Even though it cost them everything in this world, they knew they would gain everything in eternity.

In today's reading, Paul looked his own death in the face as he wrote to Timothy from prison, and he more or less concluded, "I don't regret suffering for the gospel, and you won't either. Run toward Jesus and remain faithful to Him. He is worth it all."

This was the fourth time recorded in Scripture that Paul had been imprisoned for his faith. In 2 Corinthians 11:23, Paul referred to having *"far more imprisonments"* than his opponents, so there may have been more than four total. Yet many in the Church were ashamed that one of their most prominent leaders was sitting in a jail cell, so they abandoned him. Second Timothy 1:15 says this included Phygelus and Hermogenes (probably former friends of Paul and Timothy's) and the church in Asia (modern-day Turkey).

Timothy may have been tempted to feel shame about Paul's situation too. But Paul told Timothy, *"Do not be ashamed of the testimony about our Lord, nor of me his prisoner, but share in suffering for the gospel by the power of God"* (2 Timothy 1:8).

Read Mark 8:38. What did Jesus say will happen to those who are ashamed of Him?

Take a look at 2 Timothy 1:9-10 again. Why do we have no reason to be ashamed of Christ?

Christ abolished death! It is our honor to share His message of salvation. And Paul was proud of the gospel — that's for sure. In Romans 1:16, he said, *"I am not ashamed of the gospel, for it is the power of God for salvation to everyone who believes."* And here in 2 Timothy 1:12b, he gave another reason: *"I am not ashamed, for I know whom I have believed, and I am convinced that he is able to guard until that day what has been entrusted to me."*

Paul knew Christ, whom he was serving. The more we know Jesus and His heart of grace for us and for others, any shame we feel will begin to dissipate. Like Paul, we won't get our confidence from ourselves but from our close relationship with God.

How might a closer relationship with God decrease your fear and shame and increase your courage and love for the gospel? What is a specific situation in your life where you need the kind of bravery and confidence that can only come from Him?

In 2 Timothy 1:14, Paul returned to the familiar theme of guarding the gospel: "*By the Holy Spirit who dwells within us, guard the good deposit entrusted to you.*" The gospel is to be stewarded well by believers, not watered down, complicated or distorted. Yet this is not a job for mere human beings; it can only be accomplished by the indwelling Holy Spirit. The gospel's preservation doesn't ultimately depend on people but on God Himself — and He is faithful.[1]

How does knowing that the Holy Spirit works and dwells in you give you the courage to guard and proclaim the gospel?

Finally, even after many had abandoned Paul, his friend Onesiphorus did not (2 Timothy 1:16-18). How were Onesiphorus' courageous actions an example to Timothy and to us?

Friend, if you've placed your faith in Jesus, He has given you His Holy Spirit, "*who is the guarantee of our inheritance*" (Ephesians 1:14) and sufficiently empowers us for "*life and godliness*" (2 Peter 1:3). With that kind of help, you can live boldly!

Lie that creates chaos:

A good God could never let the people He loves suffer.

Truth that brings clarity:

Suffering will occur in the lives of all believers while on earth because of the consequences of sin, but we are promised an eternity with no more death, tears or pain (Revelation 21:4).

WEEK THREE
Weekend Reflection + Prayer

This week, Paul repeated an important idea in our daily readings: the idea of protecting the gospel and also being protected by God (1 Timothy 6:20; 2 Timothy 1:12; 2 Timothy 1:14). While he may have been physically guarded in a prison, Paul had gospel guarding in mind: "*By the Holy Spirit who dwells within us, guard the good deposit entrusted to you*" (2 Timothy 1:14).

It's easy to think our ability to guard the gospel has to do with our personal skill set or talents, but it's actually not about our ability — it's about the power of the Holy Spirit living within us. Our responsibility is obedience to Him.

And 1 and 2 Timothy aren't the only places where the idea of spiritual guarding, or keeping, appears in Scripture. Here are a few other places where we see this idea:

> "*Do not be anxious about anything, but in everything by prayer and supplication with thanksgiving let your requests be made known to God. And the peace of God, which surpasses all understanding, will **guard** your hearts and your minds in Christ Jesus*" (Philippians 4:6-7, emphasis added).

> "*How can a young man keep his way pure? By **guarding** it according to your word*" (Psalm 119:9, emphasis added).

> "*Now to him who is able to **keep** you from stumbling and to present you blameless before the presence of his glory with great joy, to the only God, our Savior, through Jesus Christ our Lord, be glory, majesty, dominion, and authority, before all time and now and forever. Amen*" (Jude 1:24-25, emphasis added).

> "*Little children, **keep** yourselves from idols*" (1 John 5:21, emphasis added).

Friend, as you are guarding the gospel, God is guarding you! Rest in that promise today.

Let's pray.

Dear God, help me to know what it means to guard the gospel in my own life. Help me to guard my heart against false teaching by growing more in my love of Your Word. Give me a desire to study Scripture, know it and live it. Thank You for allowing me to be part of Your grand plan of redemption for the world. I'm so thankful for Your love, mercy and grace. In Jesus' name, amen.

NOTES

NOTES

WEEK *Four*

DAY 16 / 2 TIMOTHY 2:1-7

Paul encouraged Timothy to teach the gospel, using three examples.

To master anything – whether it's a musical instrument, an academic field of study, or a profession – takes years of practice, preparation and dedication to the craft. In today's reading, Paul reminded Timothy that doing the work of God's Kingdom also requires discipline and commitment to excellence. The Holy Spirit empowers us to grow in godliness, yet it is not an easy endeavor; it often involves hard work that requires endurance and perseverance.

> In his ministry, how was Timothy to obtain strength so he could do this hard work (2 Timothy 2:1)? How is this different from other kinds of strength we often try to rely on and live by?

Anything we do to serve God starts with the grace of Christ Jesus. Trying to strengthen ourselves will only lead to burnout and poor results. Timothy needed to remember that Jesus was the true source of his strength, and we do too.

Next, scholars note that the way Paul urged Timothy to "*entrust*" his biblical teachings to "*faithful men, who will be able to teach others also*" (2 Timothy 2:2), contrasted with the methods of false teachers who often claimed to have secret knowledge. The reference to "*faithful men*" also aligns what we learned in 1 Timothy 2-3 about character traits of those in church leadership roles. As an overseer of pastors, Timothy needed to pour sound teaching into others who would repeat the process.

> Not all believers in Christ are called to vocational ministry, but all believers are called to share the gospel and to love, serve and obey Jesus as we go about our lives. Read Matthew 28:19-20. How can you obey these instructions from Jesus in your current phase of life?

Paul gave three analogies that are meant to illustrate the Christian life: a soldier, an athlete and a farmer.

First, he called Timothy to be *"a good soldier of Christ Jesus"* (2 Timothy 2:3). Soldiers give up their personal freedom and comfort to serve others. They understand that their mission is serious and remain focused to accomplish it.

> What do you think Paul meant about the Christian life when he said, "*No soldier gets entangled in civilian pursuits, since his aim is to please the one who enlisted him*" (v. 4)? How

can we avoid entanglements?

Next, Paul spoke of the self-discipline of an athlete (v. 5). Paul would have been familiar with Greek sporting competitions, the victors of which obtained evergreen wreaths or crowns for their heads. But an athlete can't win unless they play by the rules, and the same is true for Christians. Followers of Jesus are called to godly living. While this obedience doesn't save us, it is evidence of our faith.

In 1 Corinthians 9:24-27, what else did Paul say about self-control and discipline?

Finally, Paul pointed to the humble farmer (2 Timothy 2:6). Farmers often do not get the same attention as soldiers or athletes, but they tirelessly work, plant and care for their land. So, too, believers in Christ commit ourselves to suffering and service. Like the farmer, we do "*not grow weary of doing good, for in due season we will reap, if we do not give up*" (Galatians 6:9).

How can diligently working for the gospel bring glory to God? What is one way God is calling you to greater diligence for the sake of the gospel?

Let the last verse of today's reading encourage you as a faithful student of the Bible: "*The Lord will give you understanding in everything*" (2 Timothy 2:7) as you continue to meditate on God's Word. This faithful pursuit of Him will bring you wisdom and understanding!

Lie that creates chaos:
Following Jesus will always be easy and bring success here on earth.

Truth that brings clarity:
Following Jesus wholeheartedly will take effort and sacrifice, but it results in spiritual blessings on earth and rewards in eternity.

DAY 17 / 2 TIMOTHY 2:8-13

Paul urged Timothy to remember Jesus Christ.

The average person sees hundreds, if not thousands, of advertisements each day. Our phones contain a perfect recipe of distractions — social media, search engines, shopping and so much more at our fingertips. With so much vying for our attention, it's easy to lose sight of the things that truly matter. In today's reading, Paul didn't want Timothy to forget his central reason for everything: Jesus.

Yesterday, we talked about how hard work, sacrifice and suffering are part of the Christian life, which might start to make us wonder … *Why follow Jesus anyway if it's so difficult and painful?* Today's scriptures emphasize that the blessings we receive in Christ infinitely outweigh the hardships, and the best way to remind ourselves of this is to keep Jesus — His life, death and resurrection — at the forefront of our minds. Paul's encouragement to "*remember Jesus Christ, risen from the dead*" (2 Timothy 2:8) may seem simple, but sometimes the most obvious thing is the easiest to forget.

> Think about your daily life. How often do you intentionally remember Jesus' victorious resurrection as you go about your job, your parenting, your errands, your routines? What keeps you from remembering Jesus?

Paul suffered for the gospel as he was locked up in a prison cell, but he did not despair, for "*the word of God is not bound*" (v. 9b)! Even though Paul was in chains, he knew that wouldn't stop the gospel from going forward. His suffering actually advanced God's Word; the Holy Spirit inspired Paul to write several books of the Bible from a prison cell. Today, we can see how God has used Paul's obedience, passion and commitment to the gospel to teach generations of believers in the Church.

Paul himself couldn't see the future, and he didn't know all God would do through his obedience, but he understood his suffering was not in vain. He said, "*Therefore I endure everything for the sake of the elect, that they also may obtain the salvation that is in Christ Jesus with eternal glory*" (v. 10).

> How does Paul's suffering for Christ, and the ministry that came from it, impact you today?

Consider that God also wants to use *your life* to make a lasting impact for His Kingdom! How might this reality change your prayers? Your relationships? Your work?

Read Romans 5:3-5. What does suffering produce in the life of a follower of Christ?

Many scholars suggest 2 Timothy 2:11-13 quotes part of a hymn sung in the early Church. "*If we have died with him, we will also live with him*" (v. 11) refers to dying to oneself for the sake of the gospel; "*if we endure, we will also reign with him*" (v. 12) means that even losing our lives is really no loss at all because we will reign with King Jesus in eternity (Luke 22:29-30).

What did Jesus say in Mark 8:35 about the person who loses their life for the sake of the gospel?

The second part of the hymn delivers a sobering reality: "*If we deny him, he also will deny us*" (2 Timothy 2:12). This is supported by Jesus' words, "*Whoever denies me before men, I also will deny before my Father who is in heaven*" (Matthew 10:33). A purposeful denial of Jesus as Lord will incur judgment.

But there is hope for believers because even "*if we are faithless, he remains faithful—for he cannot deny himself*" (2 Timothy 2:13). We are imperfect humans, and we have temporary lapses of faith, doubts and struggles with sin. But Jesus, the perfect One who is both fully human and fully God, is still faithful. Jesus loves us so much He took on human form and secured our eternal salvation! And we can take comfort in the fact that "*Jesus Christ is the same yesterday and today and forever*" (Hebrews 13:8). Commentator Phillip Jensen summarizes 2 Timothy 2:13 well: "The emphasis is upon the consistent faithfulness of Christ."[1]

No matter what, Jesus will be faithful to His character. As we close today's session, write a prayer of thanksgiving for His faithfulness in your own life.

Lie that creates chaos:
Like humans, God can be fickle and therefore cannot be trusted.

Truth that brings clarity:
God cannot be unfaithful to His own character, which makes Him perfectly trustworthy.

DAY 18 / 2 TIMOTHY 2:14-19

Paul said believers are to present ourselves as workers who don't need to be ashamed.

In 2015, a worldwide online phenomenon took over social media — it was simply known as "the dress." A woman in Scotland posted a photo of her blue dress with black lace. While many people saw the dress as black and blue, others insisted the dress appeared white and gold. Conditions around the photo, color perception and individual neurology caused people to perceive the dress differently.

While "the dress" controversy was lighthearted, it set up two distinct sides of an argument. In today's Scripture reading, Paul was not talking about lighthearted controversies — he was talking about debates that ran contrary to gospel Truth and distracted people from the main point: Jesus Christ came to save sinners.

In 2 Timothy 2:14, what did Paul say happens when we *"quarrel about words"*?

What is a nonessential (non-eternal) controversy that has divided people you know? How might this relate to Paul's point about the potential dangers of misleading *babble* (vv. 16-17a)?

Paul didn't want Timothy to be tempted to win the approval of others by teaching only what they wanted to hear; he wanted Timothy to be solely focused on heavenly approval. In 2 Timothy 2:15, he said, *"Do your best to present yourself to God as one approved, a worker who has no need to be ashamed, rightly handling the word of truth."*

Timothy was to seek God's approval zealously as a worker with an eternal purpose. If he rightly handled Scripture, Timothy would have no shame before God. On the other hand, false teachers were mishandling the Word, and while they may have won the approval of people, they had lost God's approval.

In what parts of your life are you tempted to seek the approval of others rather than God's approval? Do any priorities need reordering?

All Christians are called to handle God's Word rightly, meaning we take care to read and interpret it faithfully, never adding to it, subtracting from it, or trying to change its truths — even truths that challenge us. Those who teach the Word are called to an especially high level of accountability in this area, as promoting false views about Scripture *"lead[s] people into more and more ungodliness, and their talk will spread like gangrene"* (2 Timothy 2:16-17a).

Commentators point out that the medical terminology here is significant: There were no antibiotics in the first century, so the only way to treat gangrene (a fast-moving, deadly infection) was to cut off the infected body part. This suggests false teachers needed to be named and removed from the local church fellowship so heresies or lies would not spread.

Hymenaeus and Philetus, for example, were spreading lies about the resurrection of believers in Jesus (v. 18). While we don't know for sure what they taught, many scholars believe they rejected the idea of bodily resurrection for believers and viewed resurrection as merely spiritual or metaphorical, not literal. But without the doctrine of bodily resurrection, as one scholar points out, "the entire edifice of the gospel collapses."[1]

Read 1 Corinthians 15:12-19. Why is the doctrine of resurrection so vital to Christian teaching?

Despite false teachers, how does 2 Timothy 2:19 give us the confidence that the Church and the gospel will endure?

Hymenaeus and Philetus' view was built on a shaky foundation — in contrast to God's solid foundation. Matthew 7:27 illustrates that anything we build apart from God will eventually *"collaps[e] with a great crash"* (CSB), and Paul assured Timothy that heretics likewise will fail in the end. God is sovereign over those who belong to Him. It's true that humans have the responsibility to depart from sin. It's also true that God's work will prevail. In the meantime, Timothy needed to be diligent to keep himself from believing lies and to defend the Truth — and so do we.

Lie that creates chaos:
It's OK to distort the Bible to please others or ourselves.

Truth that brings clarity:
We are to do our best to please God by teaching and sharing His Word truthfully.

DAY 19 / 2 TIMOTHY 2:20-26

Paul instructed Timothy to pursue righteousness, faith, love and peace.

When hosting guests for an important occasion, most people will try to put their best foot forward. They use their best dishes and table settings and make every effort to leave a good impression. Unless they were trying to get their guests to leave early, they wouldn't use broken plates and cups — that would bring dishonor and embarrassment.

The household vessels in today's passage represent two types of people: faithful believers, who are represented through gold and silver, and unbelievers, who are represented through wood and clay. Gold and silver vessels are *"set apart as holy, useful to the master of the house, ready for every good work"* (2 Timothy 2:21). Likewise, faithful believers are precious to God, bringing honor to Him and sharing His Truth with others. Though we are sinners, we receive forgiveness through faith in Christ — yet those who don't trust in Him remain stuck in their sin, which is *"dishonorable"* (vv. 20-21).

Paul warned Timothy to separate himself from sin so he would remain pure (2 Timothy 2:22). Warren Wiersbe notes, "The name *Timothy* comes from two Greek words which together mean 'God-honoring.' Paul was encouraging Timothy to live up to his name!"[1]

> Think about your current stage of life. How is God calling you to set yourself apart and be *"ready for every good work"* (v. 21)?

In 2 Timothy 2:22, Paul told Timothy to *"flee youthful passions,"* using the Greek word *epithymia*, which referred to sinful desires in general and not just sinful sexual desires (like we might think of when we hear the word "passion" today).[2] Instead, Paul told Timothy to pursue the opposite of youthful, sinful desires: the spiritually mature virtues of *"righteousness, faith, love, and peace"* (v. 22).

> Practically, what does it look like to flee sinful desires in your own life?

Paul also wanted Timothy to pursue godly virtues in community with other followers of Jesus: *"along with those who call on the Lord from a pure heart"* (v. 22). What does this tell us about the importance of Christian friendships?

Instead of stirring up controversies and quarrels, how are servants of the Lord to address those who disagree with us (vv. 23-26)? How does this relate to our pursuit of love and peace?

The way we deliver God's Truth matters. It's possible to share Truth without kindness or tact, but often this kind of sharing is ineffective. Instead, when we communicate God's precious Truth, we are to do so with a gentle spirit. We proclaim the gospel in love, and ultimately, it is God who works in hearts to *"grant them repentance leading to a knowledge of the truth"* (v. 25).

Paul said unbelievers and those who proclaim lies about the gospel are caught in *"the snare of the devil"* (v. 26). But for everyone who is alive on earth, there is still hope that they can be set free by the Truth. How does God work through His people to accomplish this salvation?

Ephesians 4:29 says, *"Let no corrupting talk come out of your mouths, but only such as is good for building up, as fits the occasion, that it may give grace to those who hear."* Let's make sure that anytime God's Truth comes out of our mouths (which hopefully happens often!), it is seasoned with the grace of Jesus Christ.

Lord, we pray the words we speak will bring You honor today.

Lie that creates chaos:
We don't need to worry about being unkind as long as we are sharing Truth.

Truth that brings clarity:
Kindness is evidence of the Holy Spirit's work in our lives. When we proclaim the Truth in love, it brings Christ honor.

DAY 20 / 2 TIMOTHY 3:1-9

Paul warned Timothy about the conduct of false teachers in the last days.

We don't have to look very far to see evidence that we live in a fallen world. Each day, the news is filled with one heartbreaking story after another, many of which are caused by humanity's own sin and lies. And it only seems to get worse.

In today's reading, Paul echoed this sentiment, warning Timothy that *"the last days"* will be difficult, especially because the conduct of unbelievers and hypocritical false teachers will increasingly get worse (2 Timothy 3:1). These people described in verses 2-5 are not Christians who struggle with sin — which we all do — but people who live in open rebellion against God and His Word.

Many commentators define *"the last days"* (v. 1) as an era that started at the first coming of Jesus Christ and that will culminate in His return. Others may say this era started with the coming of the Holy Spirit after Jesus' resurrection (Acts 2), or with the destruction of Jerusalem's temple in A.D. 70, and will end with Christ's return. Either way, this means Paul, Timothy and all of us are living in the last days. So we need to remain alert.

> Paul gave Timothy a long list of characteristic sins that people in the last days will exhibit (2 Timothy 3:2-5). Some of these characteristics may seem surprising. Which one(s) stand out to you, and why?

Some commentators note that of the 18 characteristics Paul mentioned here, there is an emphasis on loving the wrong things: *"lovers of self, lovers of money ... not loving good ... lovers of pleasure rather than lovers of God"* (vv. 2-4). This problem starts in the heart.[1]

> Read Matthew 22:34-40. What is the proper order for prioritizing what we love, and why do you think Jesus said all of Scripture depends on these priorities?

Second Timothy 3:5 says some will have *"the appearance of godliness, but den[y] its power."* This means they do not have the power of God in their lives because they do not trust in Jesus and therefore don't experience the indwelling of the Holy Spirit. We know the Spirit of God brings a love for righteousness and gives believers power to turn from sin, *"for God gave us a spirit not of fear but of power and love and self-control"* (2 Timothy 1:7).

Read 2 Timothy 3:5b alongside Romans 16:17-18. How are we to interact (or not interact) with false teachers? Why is this important?

How does the Holy Spirit empower us for godly living even when false teachers oppose our faith? (Read John 16:13-15 and John 14:26 for more on the Spirit's ministry!)

In his words of warning, Paul also said false teachers "*creep into households and capture weak women, burdened with sins*" (2 Timothy 3:6). Many scholars believe this comment was directed at a group of women in Ephesus who were straying into either 1) asceticism or 2) antinomianism, the teaching that sinning is permissible because God will forgive us anyway.[2] Those who fall victim to such false teachings are stuck in confusion, "*always learning and never able to arrive at a knowledge of the truth*" (v. 7).

When have you been tempted to pursue a worldly philosophy or idea that promised to lead to knowledge but only left you feeling empty and confused? How did God bring you back to the Truth?

Despite the dangerous allure of false teachers, Paul didn't want Timothy to be fearful about them and their growing popularity — because "*their folly will be plain to all*" in the end (v. 9). Jannes and Jambres, mentioned in verse 8, were Egyptian magicians who opposed Moses in Pharaoh's court back in the Old Testament, but they ultimately looked foolish because their magic paled in comparison to God's power (Exodus 7:10-12). It's like Paul was telling Timothy, "My son, don't worry — these teachers won't win because they do not stand on the Truth."

Friend, when the world feels chaotic, we don't have to despair. We know our Lord Jesus Christ will be victorious. Rest in that promise today.

Lie that creates chaos:
False teachers may one day destroy God's Church completely.

Truth that brings clarity:
False teaching is anything but harmless — yet God's Truth prevails, and He preserves His Church.

WHO'S WHO IN 1 + 2 TIMOTHY

We've learned a lot about Paul and Timothy throughout our study, but Paul's letters also mention several other people. Read the chart below for a little more information about individuals named in 1 and 2 Timothy.

Person(s)	Reference	More Details
HYMENAEUS + ALEXANDER	1 Timothy 1:20	They were "handed over to Satan that they may learn not to blaspheme" (1 Timothy 1:20), which meant they were removed from communing with their local church in hopes that the discipline would bring repentance.
LOIS + EUNICE	2 Timothy 1:5	Lois, Timothy's grandmother, and Eunice, Timothy's mother, are mentioned as part of his spiritual heritage. Both women were Jewish believers in Christ, and both women modeled "sincere faith" (2 Timothy 1:5). They may have come to faith in Christ during Paul's ministry in Lystra (Acts 14). Lois and Eunice taught Timothy the Scriptures and the gospel from an early age, laying a firm foundation of faith for his ministry. (Never underestimate the impact of godly, prayerful, Bible-teaching grandmas and moms!)
PHYGELUS + HERMOGENES	2 Timothy 1:15	These people are not mentioned anywhere else in the Bible, so we know little about them. They turned away from Paul, possibly because they were ashamed of his trouble with the law.
ONESIPHORUS	2 Timothy 1:16–18	He was not ashamed of Paul's chains and went out of his way to find and refresh his friend. Paul prayed that Onesiphorus would "find mercy from the Lord on that day!" (2 Timothy 1:18). This refers to the Day of Judgment when all will stand before Christ. Some scholars believe Onesiphorus lost his life after helping Paul, but no one knows for certain.
HYMENAEUS + PHILETUS	2 Timothy 2:17	It's likely this is the same Hymenaeus named in 1 Timothy 1:20, though this is the only time we hear about Philetus in Scripture. Both men falsely taught that the resurrection of the dead had already taken place. They may have taught that salvation brings only a spiritual resurrection, not a physical one. Warren Wiersbe says, "The denial of a physical resurrection is a very serious thing … for it involves the resurrection of Christ and the completion of God's plan of salvation for His people."¹

Person(s)	Reference	More Details
JANNES + JAMBRES	2 Timothy 3:8	These two were not contemporaries of Paul and Timothy but of Moses. The names Jannes and Jambres do not appear anywhere else in the Bible, but Jewish tradition and writings suggest they were among the magicians in Pharaoh's court who opposed Moses in Exodus 7.
DEMAS	2 Timothy 4:10	Demas was faithful for a little while, but when the going got tough, he abandoned Paul. Paul once called Demas one of his *"fellow workers"* (Philemon 1:24), and Demas sent greetings along with Paul to the church in Colossae (Colossians 4:14). But 2 Timothy 4:10 says he later fell *"in love with this present world"* and left Paul for Thessalonica.
CRESCENS	2 Timothy 4:10	All we know about Crescens is that Paul sent him to Galatia. He was faithful to serve when Paul needed him.
TITUS	2 Timothy 4:10	Paul sent Titus to minister in Crete (Titus 1:5), similar to how he sent Timothy to minister in Ephesus. Paul's letter to Titus (what we know as the biblical book of Titus) is sometimes grouped with 1 and 2 Timothy as a "pastoral epistle." In 2 Timothy, Paul sent Titus to Dalmatia.
LUKE	2 Timothy 4:11	Luke wrote the Gospel of Luke and the book of Acts and traveled with Paul, recording his journeys. Many believe 2 Timothy was dictated by Paul to Luke.
MARK	2 Timothy 4:11	Also known as John Mark, a relative of Barnabas, he ministered with Paul on his first missionary journey. His desertion of Paul on this trip caused Paul and Barnabas to have split opinions about whether to take Mark on another trip. Mark later showed growth, and Paul said he was *"very useful... for ministry"* (2 Timothy 4:11). As best we can tell, Mark also wrote the Gospel of Mark.
TYCHICUS	2 Timothy 4:12	Paul sent Tychicus to Ephesus, which many scholars think was to relieve Timothy so he could see Paul in Rome before Paul's execution.

CARPUS	2 Timothy 4:13	He was a faithful believer located in Troas who helped Paul by showing him hospitality. Paul left his cloak, books and parchments with Carpus; he must have been a trustworthy man because these items would have been costly and important to Paul.
ALEXANDER THE COPPERSMITH	2 Timothy 4:14	Alexander was an opponent of the gospel and Paul. Some scholars think he may have been the reason for Paul's arrest, noting that a coppersmith may not have been a fan of someone shrinking his idol-making business.[2] He may also be the Alexander mentioned in 1 Timothy 1:20.
PRISCA + AQUILA	2 Timothy 4:19	Prisca (Priscilla) and Aquila were longtime, close friends of Paul and prominent figures in the church of Corinth. They also shared Paul's profession of tentmaking. For more on Prisca and Aquila, go to Page 112 of this guide.
ERASTUS	2 Timothy 4:20	Erastus may have been the treasurer of the church in Corinth (Romans 16:23) and worked with Timothy in Macedonia (Acts 19:22).
TROPHIMUS	2 Timothy 4:20	Trophimus was sick when Paul left him in Miletus. God performed many healing miracles through Paul, but His plan for Trophimus (at least in this instance) apparently did not include physical healing.
EUBULUS, PUDENS, LINUS + CLAUDIA	2 Timothy 4:21	Of the final four people mentioned in 2 Timothy, historians don't know much. Some scholars suggest Linus was the Apostle Peter's successor as the leader of the church in Rome.[3]

WEEK FOUR

Weekend Reflection + Prayer

Standing on the Truth of God includes being honest before God about our own sin and responding to His grace with repentant hearts. When King David repented of his sins against a woman named Bathsheba, he said, *"Create in me a clean heart, O God, and renew a right spirit within me"* (Psalm 51:10). To repent means to confess our sins before God, feel genuine remorse, and take steps to turn from our errors.

Part of the problem with the false teachers in 1 and 2 Timothy was they had not taken an honest look at the way they were living. Instead, they settled for *"the appearance of godliness, but denying its power"* (2 Timothy 3:5). If we're honest, we can all admit that at times, we, too, have been guilty of pretending to be more righteous than we are.

Thankfully Paul said in 2 Corinthians 7:10 that *"godly grief produces a repentance that leads to salvation without regret."* In other words, when we trust in Jesus and live with concern for His approval, we grieve with the Lord when we fall short of obeying Him — but this conviction of sin leads us to eternal life. Meanwhile, *"worldly grief produces death"* (2 Corinthians 7:10). The ungodly grieve not over their sin but over earthly things, like losing the world's approval, and this unrepentance leads to death.

As we cultivate godliness in our lives, regular and specific repentance will become a holy habit. Dear friend, you will never regret asking God to make your heart clean before Him.

Let's pray.

Dear God, I fall short every day, but You extend forgiveness and welcome me back with Your unending grace. Help me to cultivate a habit of daily repentance that brings me closer to You. Open my eyes to any sin in my life, and help me to extend forgiveness to those who have sinned against me. Thank You for sending Jesus to rescue me from my sin and bring me back into right relationship with You. Sanctify me, making me pure and righteous, in the Truth of Your Word (John 17:17). In Jesus' name, amen.

NOTES

NOTES

WEEK *Five*

DAY 21 / 2 TIMOTHY 3:10-17

Paul declared that all Scripture is breathed out by God.

Anne van der Bijl, a Dutch evangelical missionary better known as Brother Andrew, devoted his life to smuggling Bibles into the hands of persecuted people living in communist countries. "I promised God that as often as I could lay my hands on a Bible, I would bring it to these children of his behind the wall that men built," he once said, "to every … country where God opened the door long enough for me to slip through."[1]

For decades, Brother Andrew willingly put himself in harm's way because he believed in the power of the Bible to transform lives. In today's reading, we will learn about that power. God's Word is such a precious gift.

Paul also willingly put himself in harm's way to share God's Truth, living faithful to the gospel message and inviting Timothy (and us) to follow his example. God had rescued Paul when he faced persecution "*at Antioch, at Iconium, and at Lystra*" (2 Timothy 3:11) — but that doesn't mean Paul didn't suffer. He survived stoning in Lystra, and it's possible Timothy witnessed this event since it occurred in his hometown (Acts 14:19-20; Acts 16:1).[2]

> God preserved Paul's life through many persecutions. Paul continued to share the very gospel that made him the target of persecution. Why do you think he was so motivated to continue?

> What does 2 Timothy 3:12-14 say about "*all who desire to live a godly life*"? How does this apply to you and other believers you know, and how do you "*continue in what you have learned*"?

Most of us would prefer that godliness led to an easy path through life, but even Jesus Himself said, "*If the world hates you, know that it has hated me before it hated you … If they persecuted me, they will also persecute you*" (John 15:18-20b). Paul knew the weight of this suffering for the gospel, and he did not take it lightly. But he encouraged Timothy to remember what he had learned through Paul's instruction and testimony and through Scripture.

Look at 2 Timothy 3:15. When was Timothy introduced to "*the sacred writings*"? (In Timothy's case, this included the Old Testament and perhaps some early New Testament writings.[3]) What did Scripture make him "*wise for,*" and how does Scripture do the same for us today?

Here comes the fun part: We can "*come to the knowledge of the truth*" (1 Timothy 2:4) through Scripture because God Himself speaks to us through His Word!

Paul wrote, "*All Scripture is breathed out by God and profitable for teaching, for reproof, for correction, and for training in righteousness*" (2 Timothy 3:16). The Greek word for "*breathed out*" is *theopneustos,* which can also mean "divinely inspired." The Holy Spirit inspired Paul and the other biblical writers to write His Word. Therefore, the Bible is authoritative, true, perfect and powerful and can be trusted completely.

Why do you think Paul included words like "*reproof*" and "*correction*" when describing God's Word instead of just telling us it's encouraging? How does this shape your reading of Scripture?

The Bible provides everything we need to be "*equipped for every good work*" (2 Timothy 3:17) and is sufficient in its instruction. Second Peter 1:3 reinforces this truth with the incredible promise that "*his divine power has granted to us all things that pertain to life and godliness, through the knowledge of him who called us to his own glory and excellence.*"

How has God spoken to you through His Word lately? What is one passage or verse that is special to you and reminds you to trust God's Word?

God's Word is our road map to godliness, a lamp to our feet and a light to our path (Psalm 119:105).

Lie that creates chaos:

The Bible is just a book written by men; it's old-fashioned and not trustworthy.

Truth that brings clarity:

The Bible was written by men who were inspired by the Holy Spirit. It is God's holy Word, transforming lives in all generations and cultures.

"ALL SCRIPTURE IS *breathed* OUT BY GOD AND PROFITABLE FOR TEACHING, FOR REPROOF, FOR CORRECTION, AND FOR TRAINING IN *righteousness*."

2 TIMOTHY 3:16

The upper chamber of the Mamertine prison, where prisoners were brought to wait just prior to their executions.

PAUL'S PRISON CELL IN ROME

In Rome, it is possible to visit the Mamertine Prison, which is where Paul may have awaited his final trial and execution and is likely where he wrote 2 Timothy. Some scholars believe the Apostle Peter was imprisoned there, too, but it is difficult to know for sure. The upper chamber was where prisoners on death row awaited their fate.

Today, people tour the prison to get a glimpse of history, but in the first century, it was just a dark, dirty and depressing dungeon.[1] Picturing Paul writing to Timothy from this cell is humbling and gives greater weightiness to his words about enduring suffering for the sake of the gospel — he was living them out. But he knew his suffering was preparing him for *"an eternal weight of glory beyond all comparison"* (2 Corinthians 4:17).

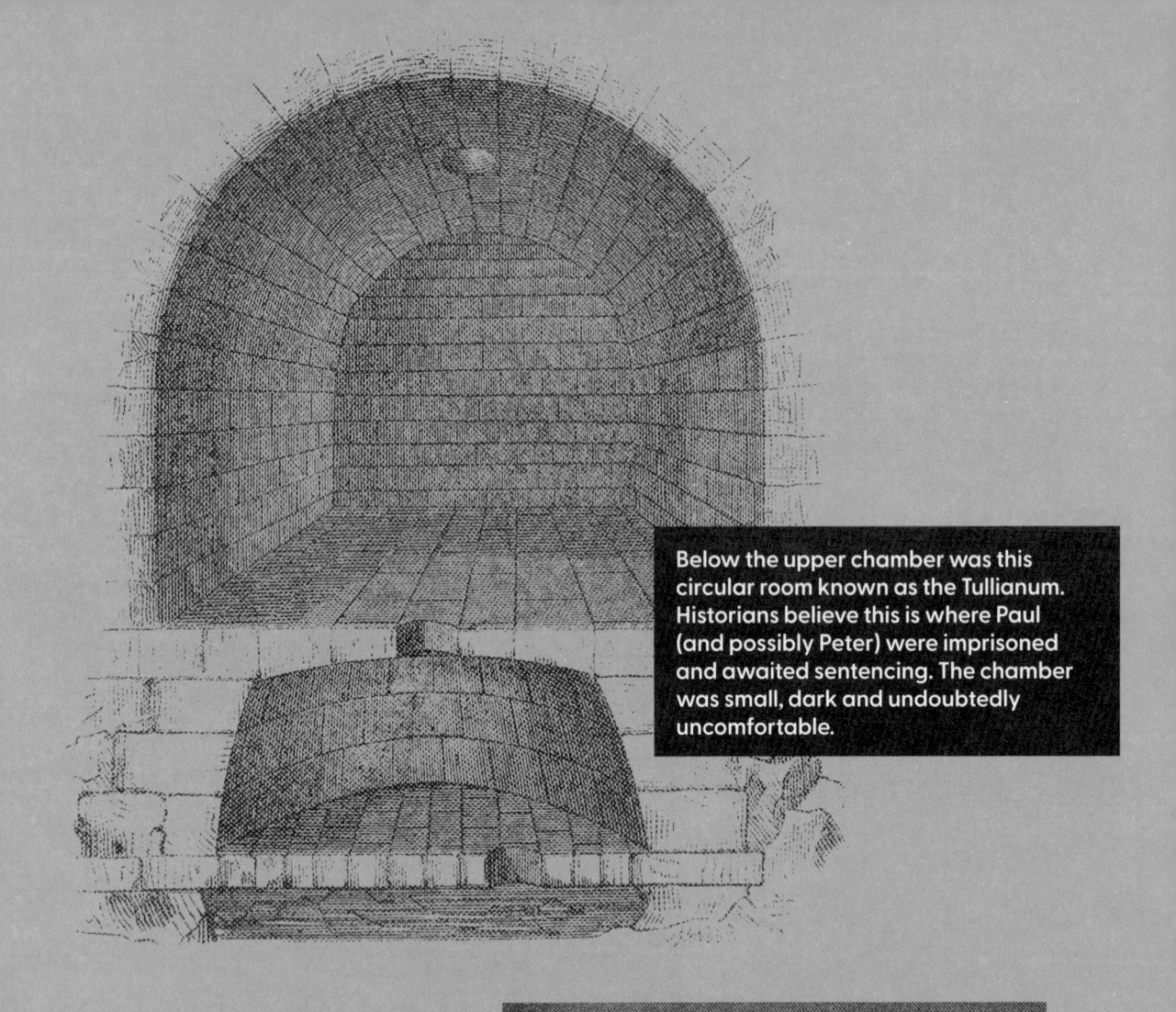

Below the upper chamber was this circular room known as the Tullianum. Historians believe this is where Paul (and possibly Peter) were imprisoned and awaited sentencing. The chamber was small, dark and undoubtedly uncomfortable.

Before stairs were installed in Mamertine, prisoners were lowered into the lower chamber through this hole.[2]

DAY 22 / 2 TIMOTHY 4:1-5

Paul told Timothy to preach God's Word.

In a relay, each runner holds a baton as they run their leg of the race, passing it on to the next runner as they finish their portion. If the baton is dropped during the exchange, the relay team will be disqualified. Passing the baton must be done with care and precision.

In today's passage, Paul was getting ready to pass the baton to Timothy, but he had one last charge for him: "*Preach the word*" (2 Timothy 4:2), he said, "*in the presence of God and of Christ Jesus,*" who will return to establish His eternal Kingdom and judge all people (2 Timothy 4:1).

The Greek word for "*preach*" in verse 2 is *kerysso*, and it means "to herald or announce." In ancient cultures, a herald was a messenger from a king or ruler, sent to give announcements and proclamations in the public square. These heralds were to speak loudly, clearly and simply on behalf of the ruler who sent them, repeating the message they had been given to as many people as possible. Changing the message in any way would have been a serious offense. And the same is true for heralds of the gospel, faithful messengers sharing God's message to everyone who will listen.

> If someone asked you to share the gospel in a few sentences, what would you say? To be good heralds, we need to know our message!

Here's one way to summarize the gospel: God made the world good, but all of us have broken God's commands (and His heart!). Since He is a good Judge, He can't simply overlook wrongdoing, and our crimes deserve a death sentence. But He also loves us all so much that while remaining fully God, He came to earth as the man Jesus Christ and died on the cross as a payment for our sin. Three days later, He rose from the dead so that all who turn from sin to faith in Jesus will live forever, trusting in His goodness and not our own.

> Timothy was to "*be ready*" to preach this Truth "*in season and out of season*" (v. 2), meaning when it was convenient and when it was not. How can you, too, be ready to share the gospel, even when it's inconvenient?

When Timothy preached the Word, it would "*reprove*" or correct those in error, "*rebuke*" by exposing sin in the lives of hearers, and "*exhort*" or encourage people to live faithfully (v. 2). All of these are important and necessary! But they can come with some discomfort.

> Why do you think people are tempted "*not [to] endure sound teaching*" from God's Word (v. 3)?

> We often think about reproof or rebuke as negative, but in Revelation 3:19, Jesus says, "*Those whom I love, I reprove and discipline, so be zealous and repent.*" How have godly reproof and rebuke been helpful or positive in your life?

Paul warned Timothy that people will have "*itching ears*," meaning they will want to listen to the teachers who most appeal to their sensibilities instead of the ones who declare God's Truth and confront their sin (2 Timothy 4:3). Of course, it's important for teachers to speak biblical Truth in a relevant, accessible way, which may mean using different teaching methods, vocabulary or examples to engage different audiences — but the gospel itself never changes. The gospel isn't always the most popular message, and people may say they want something new or different, but there is no new Truth.

> How have you been tempted to water down or soften the message of the Bible to make it appeal to others — or yourself?

> What are some reasons why people may "*turn away from listening to the truth and wander off into myths*" (v. 4)? Consider writing a prayer below for someone you know who is currently wandering from the Lord, and ask God to draw them back to Himself.

Timothy's calling was simple but not easy. To be effective for God's Kingdom, he needed to stay singularly focused on the task at hand: "*Always be sober-minded, endure suffering, do the work of an evangelist, fulfill your ministry*" (2 Timothy 4:5).

Each Christian is called to herald the true gospel, not changing it to suit ourselves or our hearers but accurately sharing the precious message God has given us. This was Timothy's charge, and it's our charge too.

Lie that creates chaos:
Scripture can mean what we want it to mean.

Truth that brings clarity:
Teachers are called to preach God's Word accurately and truthfully. Christians don't change the meaning of the Word of God to suit our lives but rather adjust our lives to God's Word.

DAY 23 / 2 TIMOTHY 4:6-8

Paul had finished the race and fought the good fight.

At this point in our study of 1 and 2 Timothy, we know Paul was likely nearing his execution date — and we may even have tears in our eyes as we read today's scriptures. Paul knew his death was imminent, but his mission was nearly complete.

He had been "*poured out as a drink offering*" before God (2 Timothy 4:6), a metaphor that referenced the Old Testament sacrificial system. When an animal was sacrificed, wine was often poured out at the base of the altar as part of the offering (e.g., Exodus 29:40; Leviticus 23:13; Numbers 15:5-12; Numbers 28:7). The image of being poured out shows us Paul gave everything he had to worship Jesus and spread the gospel.

What did Jesus say in Matthew 10:38-39 about followers who lose their lives for his sake?

How does it make you feel that Paul was awaiting his own "*departure,*" or death, with expectation and hope (2 Timothy 4:6)?

Paul returned to familiar illustrations in 2 Timothy 4:7, starting with "*I have fought the good fight.*" Paul used athletic metaphors once again here, comparing himself first to a boxer or fighter to demonstrate his tireless service to Jesus. He was beaten, lashed and stoned; endured riots; was shipwrecked; went to prison multiple times; faced hunger and thirst; lacked clothing; and endured so much more for Christ's sake — but he still kept fighting (2 Corinthians 11:23-28).

In what areas of your life can you fight "*the good fight*" (2 Timothy 4:7) in the name of Jesus?

In his second illustration, Paul said he "*finished the race*" (v. 7). Some commentators note that Paul didn't say he *won* the race, just that he finished it; he wasn't bragging but rather celebrating how God had sustained him.[1] In Acts 20:24, Paul told the Ephesian elders what his life's goal was: "*I do not account my life of any value nor as precious to myself, if only I may finish my course and the ministry that I received from the Lord Jesus, to testify to the gospel of the grace of God.*" Paul kept his eyes on the prize and finished strong!

> Paul had a spiritual goal to testify to the gospel of God's grace in his life. What are your spiritual goals, and how do you see yourself making progress toward those goals?

Paul knew his sacrifice was worth it. He would receive "*the crown of righteousness*" given by Jesus Himself (2 Timothy 4:8). In Greco-Roman culture, the victor's crown, made from laurel leaves, was awarded to champion athletes. But here Paul was not boasting in himself — He was boasting in Jesus' redeeming work in his life and the lives of "*all who have loved his appearing*" (v. 8).

> First Peter 1:4 says believers have "*an inheritance that is imperishable, undefiled, and unfading, kept in heaven.*" How can we focus on this truth — that we have a reward in heaven — even as we go about our everyday lives?

Friend, by faith, we will receive the reward of Jesus' righteousness just like Paul. Our Savior has proclaimed victory over death, so we have victory over it too. As we close today's session, ask Him for the endurance you need to run and finish your race with your eyes focused on Him.

Lie that creates chaos:
We should live for today and not care about tomorrow.

Truth that brings clarity:
All who follow Christ have a heavenly reward waiting for them — the crown of righteousness — and we live in light of eternity.

ATHLETIC IMAGERY IN THE NEW TESTAMENT

In the 1924 Olympics, a Scottish runner named Eric Liddell made headlines when he declined to run his best event, the 100-meter race, because it was scheduled on a Sunday, and he didn't want anything to come between him and worshipping the Lord. Instead, he focused on the 400-meter race, an event where he had never been as successful. But when race day came, he not only won the gold medal — he set a world record.

Liddell later went on to become a missionary to China and ultimately died in a Japanese internment camp during World War II at the age of 44. He was a gold medalist at the Olympics, but more importantly, he finished the race of life with victory in Christ Jesus.[1]

Liddell is a good example of what it means to train ourselves for godliness (1 Timothy 4:7). While the world was thinking about the reward of a gold medal at the end of a race, he was thinking about a heavenly reward at the end of his life. His training in godliness gave him endurance to persevere in serving Christ through years in an internment camp, and like Paul, he finished well.

In various places in the New Testament, we find the imagery of athletic competition as a metaphor for a faithful Christian life:

- "However, I consider my life worth nothing to me; my only aim is to finish the race and complete the task the Lord Jesus has given me—the task of testifying to the good news of God's grace" (Acts 20:24, NIV).

- "Holding fast to the word of life, so that in the day of Christ I may be proud that I did not run in vain or labor in vain" (Philippians 2:16).

- "Not that I have already obtained this or am already perfect, but I press on … forgetting what lies behind and straining forward to what lies ahead, I press on toward the goal for the prize of the upward call of God in Christ Jesus" (Philippians 3:12-14).

- "I went up because of a revelation and set before them … the gospel that I proclaim among the Gentiles, in order to make sure I was not running or had not run in vain" (Galatians 2:2).

- "*Rather train yourself for godliness; for while bodily training is of some value, godliness is of value in every way, as it holds promise for the present life and also for the life to come*" (1 Timothy 4:7b-8).

- "*An athlete is not crowned unless he competes according to the rules*" (2 Timothy 2:5).

- "*I have fought the good fight, I have finished the race, I have kept the faith. Henceforth there is laid up for me the crown of righteousness ...*" (2 Timothy 4:7-8).

- "*Do you not know that in a race all the runners run, but only one receives the prize? So run that you may obtain it. Every athlete exercises self-control in all things. They do it to receive a perishable wreath, but we an imperishable. So I do not run aimlessly; I do not box as one beating the air*" (1 Corinthians 9:24-26).

- "*Therefore, since we are surrounded by so great a cloud of witnesses, let us also lay aside every weight, and sin which clings so closely, and let us run with endurance the race that is set before us, looking to Jesus, the founder and perfecter of our faith ...*" (Hebrews 12:1-2).

Before the race even starts, runners train their bodies for competition. Good training requires focus, commitment, self-discipline and a willingness to push through pain when things get hard. Runners who have completed a proper training regimen will also be able to withstand fatigue, giving them endurance to finish well. Paul compared this process to spiritual growth. As we train ourselves in the Truth of God's Word, we become more like Jesus and grow closer to Him, even as we navigate painful realities and obstacles throughout our lives on earth. The biblical word for this lifelong process is "sanctification."

In Greek culture, the winner of an athletic competition was awarded a crown that was highly prized.[2] Christians run for a different and better prize, an imperishable *"crown of righteousness"* waiting in heaven for us (2 Timothy 4:8).

DAY 24 / 2 TIMOTHY 4:9-18

Paul gave Timothy instructions to come to him soon.

We're getting close to the end of our journey through Paul's letters to Timothy, and now Paul wanted Timothy to come quickly (2 Timothy 4:9) because he knew he didn't have much time left. He wanted his "*child in the faith*" (1 Timothy 1:2) to be by his side when the end finally came.

Paul also listed some updates about other people in the Church in these final verses, most of whom had abandoned him in his greatest need. For instance, Demas was likely the same man mentioned in Colossians 4:14 and Philemon 1:24 as a co-worker in ministry, but here we learn he fell "*in love with this present world*" and "*deserted*" Paul (2 Timothy 4:10).

> Paul lived with eternity in mind, always "*forgetting what lies behind and straining forward to what lies ahead*" (Philippians 3:13). How does this contrast with what we know about Demas' life?

On a more hopeful note, Paul's request to "*get Mark*" (2 Timothy 4:11) is a story of redemption and reconciliation. Also known as John Mark, this man accompanied Paul and Barnabas on their first missionary journey (Acts 13:5). But because John Mark abandoned them along the journey, Paul refused to take him on another mission (Acts 15:36-40). Even though a young Mark once deserted Paul, he had now evidently grown in Christian maturity, and Paul recognized "*he is very useful to me for ministry*" (2 Timothy 4:11).

> Traditionally, John Mark is also credited as the author of the Gospel of Mark. How does this remind you that God's grace can redeem even our most embarrassing failures?

In verse 13, we're not sure what Paul's books and parchments contained, but they may have been earlier writings or copies of Scripture. Scholars suggest these important Christian materials needed to be guarded, fitting into the theme of Paul's instructions to Timothy.[1]

> Paul never stopped learning from and protecting God's Word, even in his final days. What does that tell us about the importance of continuing to learn more about God and Scripture?

Paul was abandoned by his companions at his trial, yet he said, *"May it not be charged against them!"* (v. 16b). He didn't hold a grudge; he chose to forgive! What example does that give us for how to treat our brothers and sisters in Christ even when they disappoint us?

Though people abandoned Paul, God did not. In verse 17, Paul was probably not talking about God literally rescuing him from the mouth of a lion (since Roman citizens like Paul legally could not be thrown to the lions), but God certainly had saved Paul's life on multiple occasions. And Paul declared confidently that *"the Lord will rescue me from every evil deed and bring me safely into his heavenly kingdom"* (v. 18).

Paul knew this was likely the end of his earthly life, but God had rescued him from the consequences of sin, so he firmly believed death would actually bring the final victory — eternal life in God's Kingdom.

> Elsewhere, Paul once wrote *"to live is Christ, and to die is gain"* (Philippians 1:21). Alongside 2 Timothy 4:18, how does this shape our own view of death as Christians?

Friend, because Jesus defeated sin, death does not have the final word. For believers, death is a loss in the short term, and we grieve the absence of those who have departed from this world — but ultimately, even our own deaths become a win for us because we will spend eternity with our Savior.

Lie that creates chaos:
Death is the end because this life is all there is.

Truth that brings clarity:
Eternity is real, and for believers in Christ, the Lord will welcome us into eternal life with Him.

DAY 25 / 2 TIMOTHY 4:19-22

Paul concluded his second letter with personal greetings.

Today, we conclude our readings in 1 and 2 Timothy, which are the last known words of the Apostle Paul — and with those last words, he chose to send greetings to some of his most faithful friends in ministry. In the ancient world, it was customary to put greetings at the end of a letter, as is shown here.

First, Paul greeted Prisca (Priscilla) and Aquila, a married couple who had faithfully served alongside him in Corinth and who, like Paul, were also Jewish tentmakers expelled from Rome by Claudius (Acts 18:2-3). It was Priscilla and Aquila who *"explained … the way of God more accurately"* to a man named Apollos who was preaching an incomplete gospel (Acts 18:26), and they also *"risked their necks"* to protect Paul's life (Romans 16:4).

> It is estimated that Paul met Priscilla and Aquila around A.D. 49, and 2 Timothy was probably written around A.D. 66-67. They had been friends for nearly two decades! What does this teach us about the power of Christian friendship?

> These final verses demonstrate how much Paul valued his relationships with fellow believers: Without faithful co-laborers in the gospel, Paul couldn't have accomplished all he did. Think about the people who have encouraged you to follow Jesus. How can you encourage them in the same way?

In verse 21, Paul urged Timothy to *"come before winter,"* presumably because harsh weather conditions in the ancient world prevented both land and sea travel. If Timothy waited, it was possible they wouldn't see each other at all.

> We've learned a lot about Paul and Timothy's mentoring relationship. How can you be a faithful mentor to the next generation of believers? And like Timothy, how can you also put yourself in a situation to be guided by wise, mature Christians?

Paul's final farewell is fitting: *"The Lord be with your spirit. Grace be with you"* (v. 22). The first sentence addresses a singular "you," so it was meant as a blessing for Timothy; the last sentence addresses a plural "you," with Paul extending grace to all Christians.

In fact, Paul ended all his letters with a benediction of grace (e.g., Colossians 4:18; 1 Thessalonians 5:28; 2 Thessalonians 3:18) — which was in many ways the theme of his life. This personal touch was also an important proof that his letter was authentic.

> Let's reread 1 Timothy 1:13-15, which we studied a few weeks ago. What did God's grace do for Paul?

Since we're not told in Scripture exactly how Paul's life ended, we can only make educated guesses based on historical records. There is some evidence that Paul may have reached Spain after Rome, as he intended (Romans 15:24-25; Romans 15:28).[1] Whether or not this indeed happened, Church tradition has claimed that Paul was later tried, convicted and sentenced to death by beheading in Nero-ruled Rome sometime around A.D. 64-67.[2] What seems clear from Scripture is that Paul crossed the finish line of his faith-race unashamed of the One he dedicated his life to serve and proclaim.

As we wrap up our study together, let's pray that the Lord would give us endurance to finish our race, keeping us until the very end and helping us guard the precious gift of the gospel He's entrusted to us.

> Think back on your time spent studying 1 and 2 Timothy. What passages or ideas impacted you the most?

What confusing or chaos-causing lies have you confronted with God's Truth throughout this study? If any additional lies come to mind, write them below, and commit to search Scripture to find clarity! The Lord will be faithful to continue teaching you His Truth. Isn't He good?

Lie that creates chaos:
We don't really need fellowship with other believers.

Truth that brings clarity:
Christian friendship is valuable and helps us endure even the greatest suffering.

WEEK FIVE

Weekend Reflection + Prayer

Throughout 1 and 2 Timothy, we've seen a glimpse of the suffering Paul endured for the sake of the gospel. It's easy to believe the lie that if we're following God's will for our lives, we are always going to be successful, well-liked and untroubled. But that is not what the Bible teaches! Followers of Jesus will suffer: "*All who desire to live a godly life in Christ Jesus will be persecuted*" (2 Timothy 3:12). So if we're going to run the race of life successfully, we need endurance through times of suffering.

That endurance comes from God Himself. And He is the One who graciously inspired godly men to write the Bible so we can find the Truth in its pages. God's Word is fuel for endurance! As we spend time studying Scripture and worshipping at the feet of Jesus, may we unashamedly declare, "*I know whom I have believed, and I am convinced that he is able to guard until that day what has been entrusted to me*" (2 Timothy 1:12).

To some, it may have appeared like Paul lost the race at his execution. But the very fact that we are studying these words today means that by God's great grace, Paul successfully passed the baton of the gospel to Timothy, his true child in the faith, and it has passed from generation to generation to get to us today. Who will you pass the baton to?

Dear friend, we don't have to do life in this confusing, chaotic world all alone. Together, through faith in Christ, we can …

+ *Run the race.*
+ *Endure suffering.*
+ *Guard the gospel.*
+ *Finish strong.*
+ *Pass on Truth to the next generation.*

Because Jesus is worth it.

Let's pray.

Dear God, thank You for Your servants Paul and Timothy, whose examples of godliness still minister to us today. Help me to invest my life in the things that matter for eternity and to declare the Truth of Your gospel through my words and the testimony of my life. Strengthen me through Your Holy Spirit to fight the good fight, finish the race and keep the faith. I want to honor You in all things. In Jesus' name, amen.

NOTES

NOTES

ENDNOTES

AUTHOR AND DATE OF 1 + 2 TIMOTHY

1. *ESV Study Bible* (*The Holy Bible, English Standard Version*), Crossway, 2008.
2. Dockery, David S., editor. *Holman Bible Handbook*, Holman Bible Publishers, 1992, p. 736.
3. *ESV Study Bible* (*The Holy Bible, English Standard Version*), Crossway, 2008.

THE WORST OF SINNERS: MORE ABOUT PAUL

1. Silva, Moisés, and Merrill Chapin Tenney. *The Zondervan Encyclopedia of the Bible, M-P, Revised, Full-Color Edition*, vol. 4, Grand Rapids, MI, The Zondervan Corporation, 2009, p. 698.
2. Sproul, R.C. *The Essential Truths of the Christian Faith*, Carol Stream, IL: Tyndale Momentum, 1992, p. 277.

WHO WAS TIMOTHY? PAUL'S RELATABLE MISSIONARY ASSISTANT

1. Marty, William H. "Acts," *The Moody Bible Commentary*, Chicago, IL: Moody Publishers, 2014, p. 1707.

WHY DID PAUL WRITE 1 + 2 TIMOTHY?

1. *ESV Study Bible* (*The Holy Bible, English Standard Version*), Crossway, 2008.

GODLINESS WITH CONTENTMENT IS GREAT GAIN: THEMES IN 1 + 2 TIMOTHY

1. *ESV Study Bible* (*The Holy Bible, English Standard Version*), Crossway, 2008, p. 2322.

2. Hughes, R. Kent. "1 Timothy," *Gospel Transformation Bible: English Standard Version*, edited by Bryan Chapell and Dane Ortlund, Wheaton, IL, Crossway, 2013, p. 1627.
3. *ESV Study Bible* (*The Holy Bible, English Standard Version*), Crossway, 2008, p. 2322.

DAY 1

1. Wiersbe, Warren W. *Be Faithful: It's Always too Soon to Quit! NT Commentary: 1 & 2 Timothy, Titus, Philemon*, Colorado Springs, CO: David C Cook, 1981.

DAY 4

1. Tabb, Brian J. *1-2 Timothy and Titus, A 12-Week Study*, edited by Dane C. Ortlund, Wheaton, IL: Crossway, 2017, p. 13.
2. Wright, N.T. *1 & 2 Timothy and Titus: 12 Studies for Individuals and Groups*, Downers Grove, IL: InterVarsity Press.
3. Cobble, Tara-Leigh. *The Bible Recap: A One-Year Guide to Reading and Understanding the Entire Bible*, Minneapolis, MN: Bethany House, 2020, p. 722.
4. Cobble, Tara-Leigh. *The Bible Recap: A One-Year Guide to Reading and Understanding the Entire Bible*, Minneapolis, MN: Bethany House, 2020.
5. Cobble, Tara-Leigh. *The Bible Recap: A One-Year Guide to Reading and Understanding the Entire Bible*, Minneapolis, MN: Bethany House, 2020.

TOUGH TOPICS IN 1 TIMOTHY: ARE WOMEN SAVED IN CHILDBEARING?

1. Litfin, A. Duane. "1 Timothy," *The Bible Knowledge Commentary: An Exposition of the Scriptures*, edited by J.F. Walvoord and R.B. Zuck, vol. 2, Victor Books, 1985, p. 734.

DAY 5

1. Litfin, A. Duane. "1 Timothy," *The Bible Knowledge Commentary: An Exposition of the Scriptures*, edited by J.F. Walvoord and R.B. Zuck, vol. 2, Victor Books, 1985.

2. Jensen, Phillip D. *1 & 2 Timothy for You*, edited by Carl Laferton, Charlotte, NC: The Good Book Company, 2019, p. 69.
3. Litfin, A. Duane. "1 Timothy," *The Bible Knowledge Commentary: An Exposition of the Scriptures*, edited by J.F. Walvoord and R.B. Zuck, vol. 2, Victor Books, 1985.
4. Jensen, Phillip D. *1 & 2 Timothy for You*, edited by Carl Laferton, Charlotte, NC: The Good Book Company, 2019, p. 69.

TOUGH TOPICS IN 1 TIMOTHY: WHAT DOES THE "HUSBAND OF ONE WIFE" MEAN?

1. *ESV Study Bible* (*The Holy Bible, English Standard Version*), Crossway, 2008, p. 2329.
2. *ESV Study Bible* (*The Holy Bible, English Standard Version*), Crossway, 2008.
3. Litfin, A. Duane. "1 Timothy," *The Bible Knowledge Commentary: An Exposition of the Scriptures*, edited by J.F. Walvoord and R.B. Zuck, vol. 2, Victor Books, 1985.

DAY 6

1. Moore, Matt. *First Timothy*. Eternity Bible College, https://app.rightnowmedia.org/pt/content/details/370280.
2. Litfin, A. Duane. "1 Timothy," *The Bible Knowledge Commentary: An Exposition of the Scriptures*, edited by J.F. Walvoord and R.B. Zuck, vol. 2, Victor Books, 1985.
3. Litfin, A. Duane. "1 Timothy," *The Bible Knowledge Commentary: An Exposition of the Scriptures*, edited by J.F. Walvoord and R.B. Zuck, vol. 2, Victor Books, 1985, p. 738.

DAY 7

1. Platt, David, Daniel L. Akin, et al. *Exalting Jesus in 1 & 2 Timothy and Titus*, Nashville, TN: Holman Reference, 2013.
2. Platt, David, Daniel L. Akin, et al. *Exalting Jesus in 1 & 2 Timothy and Titus*, Nashville, TN: Holman Reference, 2013.

THE GOSPEL IN A FIRST-CENTURY HYMN

1. *ESV Study Bible* (*The Holy Bible, English Standard Version*), Crossway, 2008.

DAY 8

1. Platt, David, Daniel L. Akin, et al. *Exalting Jesus in 1 & 2 Timothy and Titus*, Nashville, TN: Holman Reference, 2013.

DAY 9

1. *ESV Study Bible* (*The Holy Bible, English Standard Version*), Crossway, 2008.

DAY 10

1. "International Widows' Day," United Nations. https://www.un.org/en/observances/widows-day.
2. Koessler, John. "1 Timothy," *The Moody Bible Commentary*, edited by M. Rydelnik and M. Vanlaningham, Chicago, IL: Moody Publishers, p. 1901.
3. "On Younger Widows," Ligonier, July 28, 2009, https://www.ligonier.org/learn/devotionals/younger-widows.

WIDOWS IN THE BIBLE

1. Platt, David, Daniel L. Akin, et al. *Exalting Jesus in 1 & 2 Timothy and Titus*, Nashville, TN: Holman Reference, 2013.

DAY 11

1. *ESV Study Bible* (*The Holy Bible, English Standard Version*), Crossway, 2008.
2. *ESV Study Bible* (*The Holy Bible, English Standard Version*), Crossway, 2008, p. 2333.
3. Platt, David, Daniel L. Akin, et al. *Exalting Jesus in 1 & 2 Timothy and Titus*, Nashville, TN: Holman Reference, 2013, p. 94.

TOUGH TOPICS IN 1 TIMOTHY: WHY DID PAUL TELL TIMOTHY TO DRINK WINE?

1. Elwell, Walter A. and Barry J. Beitzel. "Wine," *Baker Encyclopedia of the Bible*, Grand Rapids, MI: Baker Book House, 1988, p. 2147.
2. Hellie, Richard. "Slave Societies," edited by the editors of Encyclopaedia Britannica, *Encyclopaedia Britannica*, 2024. https://www.britannica.com/topic/slavery-sociology/Slave-societies.

TOUGH TOPICS IN 1 TIMOTHY: WHY DOES PAUL TALK ABOUT SLAVERY?

1. *ESV Study Bible* (*The Holy Bible, English Standard Version*), Crossway, 2008, p. 21.

DAY 13

1. Platt, David, Daniel L. Akin, et al. *Exalting Jesus in 1 & 2 Timothy and Titus*, Nashville, TN: Holman Reference, 2013, p. 122.
2. Koessler, John. "1 Timothy," *The Moody Bible Commentary*, edited by M. Rydelnik and M. Vanlaningham, Chicago, IL: Moody Publishers.

DAY 14

1. Litfin, A. Duane. "1 Timothy," *The Bible Knowledge Commentary: An Exposition of the Scriptures*, edited by J.F. Walvoord and R.B. Zuck, vol. 2, Victor Books, 1985.

DAY 15

1. Tabb, Brian J. *1-2 Timothy and Titus, A 12-Week Study*, edited by Dane C. Ortlund, Wheaton, IL: Crossway, 2017.

DAY 17

1. Jensen, Phillip D. *1 & 2 Timothy for You*, edited by Carl Laferton, The Good Book Company, 2019, p. 158.

DAY 18

1. Litfin, A. Duane. "2 Timothy," *The Bible Knowledge Commentary: An Exposition of the Scriptures*, edited by J.F. Walvoord and R.B. Zuck, vol. 2, Victor Books, 1985, p. 754.

DAY 19

1. Wiersbe, Warren W. *Be Faithful: It's Always Too Soon To Quit! NT Commentary: 1 & 2 Timothy, Titus, Philemon*, Colorado Springs, CO: David C Cook, 1981, p. 159.
2. *ESV Study Bible* (*The Holy Bible, English Standard Version*), Crossway, 2008.

DAY 20

1. Wiersbe, Warren W. *Be Faithful: It's Always Too Soon To Quit! NT Commentary: 1 & 2 Timothy, Titus, Philemon*, Colorado Springs, CO: David C Cook, 1981, p. 159
2. *ESV Study Bible* (*The Holy Bible, English Standard Version*), Crossway, 2008.

WHO'S WHO IN 1 + 2 TIMOTHY

1. Wiersbe, Warren W. *Be Faithful: It's Always Too Soon To Quit! NT Commentary: 1 & 2 Timothy, Titus, Philemon*, Colorado Springs, CO: David C Cook, 1981, p. 157.
2. Platt, David, Daniel L. Akin, et al. *Exalting Jesus in 1 & 2 Timothy and Titus*, Nashville, TN: Holman Reference, 2013.
3. Hughes, R. Kent and Bryan Chapell. *1 & 2 Timothy and Titus: To Guard the Deposit*, Wheaton, IL: Crossway Books, 2000.

DAY 21

1. Sillman, Daniel. "Died: Brother Andrew, Who Smuggled Bibles into Communist Countries." *Christianity Today*, September 27, 2022. https://www.christianitytoday.com/news/2022/september/died-brother-andrew-open-door-smuggled-bibles-into-communis.html.
2. *ESV Study Bible* (*The Holy Bible, English Standard Version*), Crossway, 2008.
3. *ESV Study Bible* (*The Holy Bible, English Standard Version*), Crossway, 2008.

PAUL'S PRISON CELL IN ROME

1. Jeter, Derrick G. "Historical Background of Paul's Final Imprisonment," *Insight for Living*, August 14, 2017, https://insight.org/resources/article-library/individual/historical-background-of-paul-s-final-imprisonment.

2. *BiblePlaces.com*, "Mamertine Prison," https://www.bibleplaces.com/mamertine-prison/.

DAY 23

1. Platt, David, Daniel L. Akin, et al. *Exalting Jesus in 1 & 2 Timothy and Titus*, Nashville, TN: Holman Reference, 2013.

ATHLETIC IMAGERY IN THE NEW TESTAMENT

1. Metaxas, Eric. *7 Men: And the Secrets to Their Greatness*, Nashville, TN: Thomas Nelson, 2015.

2. Platt, David, Daniel L. Akin, et al. *Exalting Jesus in 1 & 2 Timothy and Titus*, Nashville, TN: Holman Reference, 2013.

DAY 24

1. Platt, David, Daniel L. Akin, et al. *Exalting Jesus in 1 & 2 Timothy and Titus*, Nashville, TN: Holman Reference, 2013.

DAY 25

1. Meinardus, Otto F. "Paul's Missionary Journey to Spain: Tradition and Folklore," *Biblical Archeologist*, 1978. https://www.uni-goettingen.de/de/document/download/240d98d46822eef693484c34c5aecf0d.pdf/BA_1978-2_PaulsMissionary.pdf

2. *ESV Study Bible* (*The Holy Bible, English Standard Version*), Crossway, 2008.

ABOUT PROVERBS 31 MINISTRIES

She is clothed with strength and dignity; she can laugh at the days to come.

PROVERBS 31:25

Proverbs 31 Ministries is a nondenominational, nonprofit Christian ministry that seeks to lead women into a personal relationship with Christ. With Proverbs 31:10-31 as a guide, Proverbs 31 Ministries reaches women in the middle of their busy days through free devotions, podcast episodes, speaking events, conferences, resources, and training in the call to write, speak and lead others.

We are real women offering real-life solutions to those striving to maintain life's balance, in spite of today's hectic pace and cultural pull away from godly principles.

Wherever a woman may be on her spiritual journey, Proverbs 31 Ministries exists to be a trusted friend who understands the challenges she faces and walks by her side, encouraging her as she walks toward the heart of God.

Visit us online today at proverbs31.org!

P31 PROVERBS 31 ministries

Your next study guide is coming soon ...

FRESH START:

A Study of the Book of Genesis

Coming November 2024 to
p31bookstore.com